ROMANCES
YOU'LL NEVER GET HIM BACK, ANN. THAT LITTLE CHEAT WILL DO ANYTHING TO HOLD DICK!
BUT HE DOESN'T KNOW THE THINGS I DO ABOUT HER. JUST WAIT TILL I GET HIM ALONE!
IN THIS ISSUE: DID I GIVE MY LIPS TOO FREELY?
JUNE
VENUS
A TRUE STORY by derf
CHAPLAINS AT WAR
bravery is in the heart!
SH-T!
$3.00
Comics for ADULTS ONLY
LOOK AT A REAL BARREL O'GOODIES!
CHARLTON COMICS
JUST MARRIED
NO. 93
MAR.
ONLY 20¢
6p
SHOULD A JEWISH BOY AND AN IRISH GIRL FALL IN LOVE? BEGINNING IN THIS ISSUE THE CONTINUING STORY OF DAVID and EILEEN
TEE
ADULTS $2.00 ONLY
DELL
15¢
KOOK
M-A-A-N!!
PARALLAX
$1.00
THE GREAT SOCIETY COMIC BOOK
WHY....THAT, THAT COULD BE A GREAT SOCIETY!
by D.J. ARNESON AND TONY TALLARICO
SUPER LBJ
KING
POPEYE
PERSONAL SERVIC
CAREERS
THERE IS NOTHING LIKE A HAIRCUT, SHAVE AND MANICURE TO MAKE ME FEEL GOOD!
I HAVE A HEAVY DATE WITH OLIVE OYL TONIGHT! ARF! ARF!

HOLY SH*T!
THE WORLD'S WEIRDEST COMIC BOOKS

Also by Paul Gravett:
Manga: Sixty Years of Japanese Comics
(Laurence King/Collins Design, 2004)
The Mammoth Book of Best Crime Comics (editor)
(Robinson/Running Press, 2008)

Also by Paul Gravett and Peter Stanbury
Graphic Novels: Everything You Need to Know
(Aurum Press/Collins Design, 2005)
Great British Comics (Aurum Press, 2006)

For more about the worlds of comics visit:
www.paulgravett.com

For information, address St. Martin's Press,
175 Fifth Avenue, New York, N.Y. 10010.
www.stmartins.com

Design by Peter Stanbury

Library of Congress Cataloging-in-Publication Data
Available Upon Request

ISBN-13: 978-0-312-53395-3
ISBN-10: 0-312-53395-0

First published in Great Britain by Aurum Press Ltd. as *The Leather Nun
and Other Incredibly Strange Comics*.

First US Edition: February 2009

10 9 8 7 6 5 4 3 2 1

HOLY SH*T!

THE WORLD'S WEIRDEST COMIC BOOKS

PAUL GRAVETT & PETER STANBURY

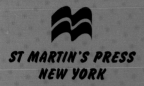

ST MARTIN'S PRESS
NEW YORK

FUNNY HA-HA OR FUNNY PECULIAR?

So how weird does a comic have to be to qualify as "the world's weirdest"? What tips it over the knife edge from making you laugh to making you squirm? Let's face it, most comics are by nature pretty darn weird. How "normal" is a child-sized rodent standing upright in gloves and short pants? Or a billionaire orphan so screwed up by seeing his parents killed as a child that he dresses up as a bat? Or a meek scientist who, when he gets tetchy, bursts out of his clothes into an angry green giant—and somehow always keeps his purple pants on? Yet we take Mickey Mouse, Batman and Hulk for granted as everyday American icons.

We're after more than regular, ordinary weirdness for this book. We want the sort of way-out concepts and characters to make you reel and wonder, "What were they *thinking*?" Cranking out story after story on America's assembly lines of mass-market comic books could drive some writers, artists, editors and publishers to absurd measures. Or, as the Fantastic Four's Thing would grumble, "Wotta revoltin' development!" Still, somebody with money must have believed that the "next big thing" was going to be a reanimated flower-power clothes dummy, or an immortal, insufferably smug gigolo, or an overweight super-glutton who can turn into a flying saucer. And can you blame them for backing the aforementioned Brother Power The Geek, Jon Juan Superlover and Fatman the Human Flying Saucer? There's really no predicting who or what will become a global superstar.

So we've not focused solely on the American mainstream; we've investigated the more neglected backwaters, bayous and black lagoons. With lots of help, we've scoured through not only all manner of American comics past and present, but also those from Britain, Canada, Australia, Mexico, Italy, Malaysia and Russia, to unearth Aborigine legends, a topless female Spider-Man and Italy's own Superman, renamed Nembo Kid.

We've also delved into the rebellious comics of the American underground movement, unshackled from the prim censors scrutinizing every bust line and shadowy crotch at the Comics Code Authority. While these "comix"—as in X-rated—first flowered in the hippy 1960s, their family tree goes back to the 1950s mail-order fetish comics of Eric Stanton and the compact "Tijuana bible" porno-parodies of the 1930s, and their influence lives on as touchstones of freedom of expression for maverick creators and publishers to this day.

And we've mined a whole other rich seam of educational and promotional comics. These strait-laced giveaways hijack the populist entertainment medium of strips to sell a product, message, faith or philosophy, from popsicles, prunes and poultry feed to the perils of smoking, communism and the Atomic Bomb. They include religious comics, which seek to convert through evangelical parables in panels or offer visions of Catholic guilt and Islamic hell. All these message comics reflect their times, as they instruct readers in how to behave and what to buy and believe. They reveal what was once the status quo and how much, or how little, values and sensibilities have shifted over the years. That's why we've also featured some comics about and by African-Americans, because they highlight how rare the prominent, positive representations of black characters have been in the predominantly white, straight, male comics industry. What's truly weird about black heroes, and indeed all minorities, in mass-produced comics has been their virtual absence.

The truth is, you can't always judge a comic by its cover, so the comics we chose had to have stories inside that were at least as strange as their covers, for you to discover. We're sure there's at least something in here that should amuse, amaze, or offend just about anyone. If anything unites these disparate, sometimes desperate outpourings it's the human imagination unleashed and driven to make a joke, a fantasy, a buck, a point, a confession, a shock, a political statement, and the fascination of seeing where all this can lead. In the end, the definition of "world's weirdest" comes down to individual taste, because, like Beauty, Weirdness is truly in the eye of the beholder. We can't help wondering if, on a parallel Earth, The Geek, Jon Juan and Fatman are household names still published today, with merchandise, theme parks and blockbuster movies of their own. How the mind boggles!

Paul Gravett & Peter Stanbury

"WHAT A FOOL I'VE BEEN! IT WAS DICK I REALLY LOVED!"

"I HAD MY OPERATION! IT WAS A SUCCESS, THEY SAID! BUT I STILL COULDN'T WALK! I DIDN'T CARE WHETHER I EVER WALKED! I LOOKED UPON MY LEGS AS THE VERY SYMBOL OF MY SHATTERED DREAMS!
PLEASE TRY, MISS HUNTER. TRY TO MOVE YOUR LEGS JUST A LITTLE?
I CAN'T I TELL YOU! I DON'T CARE IF I EVER WALK! I DON'T CARE!!

It's hard to believe that this double entendre and more inside were accidental. Once the industry appointed the Comics Code Authority as its independent regulator in 1954, such suggestive material would struggle to get past their strait-laced scrutineers. This scene links to "Magnificent Deception," a morality tale by writer Dana Dutch and artist Joe Kubert (above) about the fickleness of Hollywood fame. Torn between two lovers, budding starlet Pauline Hunter drops screenwriter Dick Palmer and marries her leading man, actor Gregory Prince, "a pompous ham" according to the spurned Dick. Tragedy strikes on Pauline's morning ride when a fall from her horse lands her in a wheelchair. What is worse, her hubby, convinced that the public will quickly forget his wife now that she is out of the limelight, callously dumps her. Realizing her mistake, Pauline finds hope and love with Dick and walks again, with him, down the aisle. Famed for his full-bodied females, ace illustrator Matt Baker was one of the few African-Americans in the industry at this time, though he seldom drew black characters.

TEEN-AGE ROMANCES NO. 9, APRIL 1950, PUBLISHED BY & © ST. JOHN PUBLICATIONS, NEW YORK, 36-PAGE COMIC. COVER BY MATT BAKER, INTERIORS BY VARIOUS ARTISTS

YOU WANT MORE? HOLLYWOOD 70 ROMANCE 24 DISABILITY 82

ANC
TEEN-AGE
ROMANCES
10¢
APRIL
YOU'LL NEVER GET HIM BACK, ANN. THAT LITTLE CHEAT WILL DO ANYTHING TO HOLD DICK!
BUT HE DOESN'T KNOW THE THINGS I DO ABOUT HER. JUST WAIT TILL I GET HIM ALONE!
IN THIS ISSUE:
DID I GIVE MY LIPS TOO FREELY?

"GET DOWN! ON YOUR STOMACHS! HIDE YOUR FACES! DON'T LOOK AT IT!"

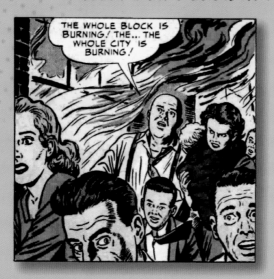

THE WHOLE BLOCK IS BURNING! THE... THE WHOLE CITY IS BURNING!

FIRE AND BLAST!

The Cold War stoked genuine fears of an atom-bomb attack on America. Would you know what to do? In this cautionary tale about being prepared, blasé Phil Smith passes up responsible Tom Walker's invitation to learn all about Civil Defense in favor of a fun afternoon at the zoo with their kids. Back for dinner, Smith panics when an A-bomb hits the city. Luckily, Tom's son Billy gets the Smiths to "duck and cover" seconds before the blast shatters the windows. With no water or extinguishers, fire rages through their building and Smith blocks vital phone lines by calling emergency services. It is only Billy's training that prevents further mishaps and saves everyone's lives. Suitably chastened, Smith resolves to take Civil Defense more seriously. This comic skirts around the perils of radiation poisoning by explaining that the explosion was not the dreaded mushroom cloud after all, but merely an accident at the city's largest industrial plant.

FIRE AND BLAST!, 1952, PRODUCED BY & © FEATURE PUBLICATIONS/PRIZE COMICS, NEW YORK, FOR THE NATIONAL FIRE PROTECTION ASSOCIATION, 16-PAGE FREE COMIC. WRITER UNCREDITED, DRAWN BY MART BAILEY

YOU WANT MORE?   ATOMIC 72   RADIATION 56   WAR 42

FIRE AND BLAST!
TOM, — IT - IT'S FRIGHTENING! WHEN I THINK THAT SOME DAY WE MAY BE UNDER AN A-BOMB ATTACK, IT MAKES MY KNEES WEAK! I FEEL SO HELPLESS!
I KNOW, MOTHER! THE THREAT OF WAR ISN'T PLEASANT! BUT WE'VE GOT TO FACE IT! WE'VE GOT TO BE READY WHEN AND IF IT DOES COME! IF WE ARE, WE'LL BE FAR FROM HELPLESS!
MART BAILEY

"WHAT'S THAT STRANGE CROSS? IT HAS HOOKS ON THE ENDS!"

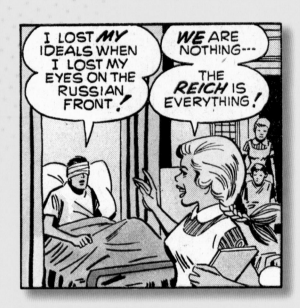

Bright little Aryan Hansi wins a contest that whisks her from her God-fearing mother to a Nazi-run academy in Prague. Here, the naïve peasant girl is indoctrinated into a blind faith in Hitler's victory and rejects the Bible, once her only reading. After Germany's defeat, she escapes from a Russian camp to the American Zone. Afraid at first that Americans are "all gum-chewing gangsters," Hansi ends up finding safety among them. When her missing German lover Rudy turns up alive, they are finally wed, but their marriage is empty until Rudy brings home a Bible. As a result, they begin a new life, saving souls in the affluent but troubled USA. Hansi converts to another form of patriotic pride, extolling now the virtues of freedom-loving America. The style is reminiscent of Archie Comics; Al Hartley was drawing for them at the time and was also able to feature Archie in several of his Christian comics.

HANSI, THE GIRL WHO LOVED THE SWASTIKA, 1976, PUBLISHED BY & © SPIRE CHRISTIAN COMICS/
FLEMING H. REVELL COMPANY, OLD TAPPAN, NEW JERSEY, 36-PAGE COMIC.
WRITTEN AND DRAWN BY AL HARTLEY FROM THE 1973 NOVEL BY & © MARIA ANNE HIRSCHMANN

YOU WANT MORE?   HITLER 64   PATRIOTISM 114   CHRISTIANITY 102

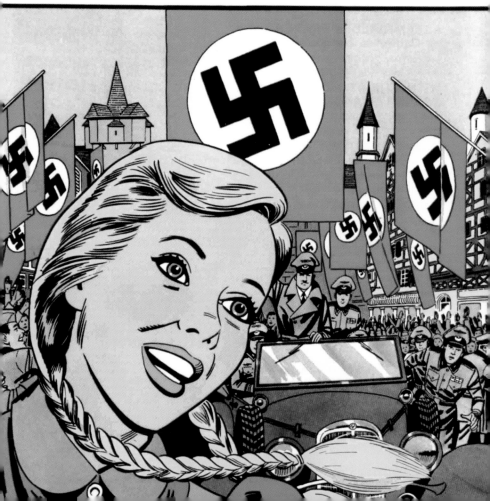

Hansi

THE·GIRL·WHO·LOVED·THE·SWASTIKA

39¢

"EXTRACT OF ANGRY GORILLA WITH BELLY OF SUNBURNT RHINO TO GIVE YOU SPEED AND POWER…"

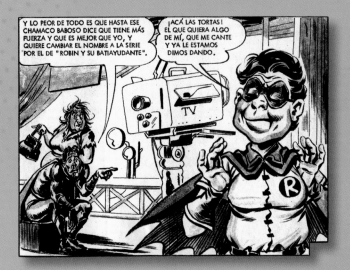

At the height of Sixties Batmania in Mexico, pop-eyed, bulbous-nosed witch Hermelinda uses her "charms" to get into the TV studio where they are filming "Badman." Seeing the vain actor behind the mask getting pulverized from doing his own stunts, she invites him over to her laboratory shack and plies him full of potions to make him invulnerable for one hour. At the next day's shoot, Badman demolishes Robin, who had threatened to steal the show from him, and then the cast, crew and set. But as his magic powers fade, his bat-rope breaks and he plummets down to earth and falls under a truck. Taking his broken body back to her lab, Hermelinda makes a "new man" of him, propped up on crutches and reduced to hawking lucky "bat-lottery" tickets. Apparently, Mexico's Public Education Department insisted that the publisher change the weekly's title, *Brujerias* ("Witchcraft"), because it promoted superstition—"real" witches were writing in for Hermelinda's recipes.

BRUJERIAS NO. 76, MARCH 18, 1967, PUBLISHED BY & © EDITORMEX MEXICANA, S.A., PORTALES, MEXICO, 36-PAGE B/W COMIC. BATMAN & ROBIN ™ & © 2008 DC COMICS. WRITTEN & DRAWN BY JOSÉ CABEZAS

YOU WANT MORE?   SUPERHEROES 38   MAGIC 78   TELEVISION 40

BRUJERIAS
REVISTA CÓMICO-SATÍRICA PARA ADULTOS
SOCK!
POW!
CRASH!
Editormex
$1.00
No. 76

"I DIDN'T ENJOY MY FIRST CIGARETTE. NO ONE DOES."

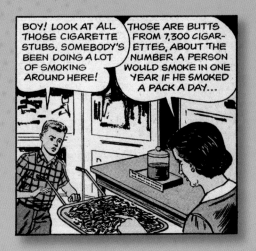

Cigarettes, once seen as a male accessory, were rebranded for women as "torches of liberty" in 1929, the same year that German physician Fritz Lickint recognized the link between smoking and lung cancer, prompting a Nazi anti-smoking campaign. In America, despite the existence of similar scientific evidence by the mid-1950s, the Surgeon General recommended smokers to give up only in 1964, but *Where There's Smoke...* started warning Americans in 1963, when the first of 24 printings and 15.3 million copies were given away. Tattle-tale Tina squeals to Mom about older brother Rickey smoking his first cigarette, peer-pressured by bad-boy Chuck. Actually, Mom is no example; she's a smoker herself, unable to quit. Next day, the boys' fitness instructor takes them to an educational exhibit. Bombarded with statistics, the kids really get the point when they see an automatic smoking machine produce the eight ounces of tar formed by smoking one pack a day for a year. Back home, when Rickey and Tina promise never to smoke, Mom vows to stop right now and chucks away her ashtrays. Tina chirps, "And now the house won't have that smokey ol' smell all the time!"

WHERE THERE'S SMOKE...THERE'S DANGER, 1963, PUBLISHED BY & © THE AMERICAN CANCER SOCIETY, 16-PAGE FREE COMIC. WRITTEN BY MALCOLM ATER SENIOR AND DRAWN BY JACK SPARLING

YOU WANT MORE?   UP IN SMOKE 76   GOOD ADVICE 54   CHILDREN 108

WHERE THERE'S SMOKE...
AMERICA
CANCER
SOCIETY

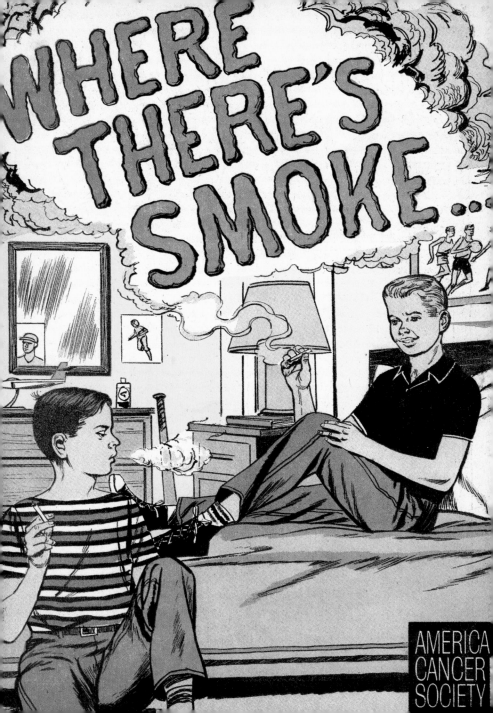

"I SHOW NO MERCY OR COMPASSION FOR AGGRESSORS...ONLY FOR THEIR VICTIMS...FOR THE INNOCENT!"

MR. A.

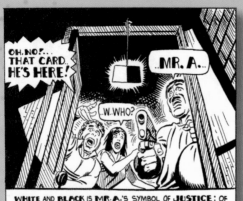

Few readers of Steve Ditko's work with co-creator Stan Lee on wisecracking *Spider-Man* and mystic *Doctor Strange* were ready for Ditko's departure from Marvel in 1966 or his solo foray, the uncompromising *Mr. A.*, named after Aristotle's formula, A is A. Debuting in Wally Wood's *witzend* No. 3 in 1967, the pure-white-suited avenger inside an implacable metal mask forces a female social worker to decide whether he should save her life or that of the client she "failed," a punk-turned-cop-killer who fatally stabbed her and now hangs from a flagpole. Her agonizing choice to save herself and let the criminal fall to his death is Mr. A.'s tough lesson that "to have sympathy for a killer is an insult to their victims." Finally free to express his worldview, Ditko created the world's first objectivist superhero, personifying the Ayn Rand philosophy he had embraced. On his calling card are only white and black, good and evil; no shades of grey allowed. As fight scenes warped into battles of ideas, dialogues into diatribes, Ditko, the Thomas Pynchon of comics, shunned all publicity to pursue his singular path. Imagining the dark side of the sober, infallible Mr. A. inspired the disturbed, disturbing Rorschach in Alan Moore and Dave Gibbons' *Watchmen*.

MR. A., 1973, PUBLISHED BY COMIC ART PUBLISHERS, BROOKLYN, NEW YORK, 40-PAGE B/W COMIC MAGAZINE. WRITTEN AND DRAWN BY & © STEVE DITKO

YOU WANT MORE?   SUPERHEROES 94 PROBLEM KIDS 100 RETRIBUTION 28

MR. A.
75¢
OUR ONLY CHOICE
..EITHER
OOD ..OR EVIL
WHEN IS A MAN TO BE JUDGED
EVIL
...RIGHT TO KILL?

"THE WORLD NEEDS TO SEE A LIVING WITNESS, NOT A GAS BAG!"

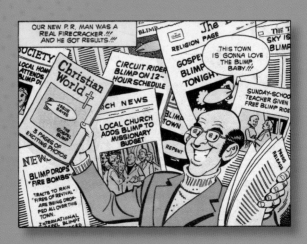

From one look at the couple next door, smoking, drinking and playing cards, "You can tell they're not Christians!!!" But how far will neighbor George and the other locals go to grab thee sinners' attention and convert them? Spying a Goodyear advertising blimp cruising above, George hits on the idea of using a blimp to display Bible verses, broadcast sermons and fire-bomb them with tracts. It's Herm who makes the blimp possible, quitting the meat-packing plant to chair a fundraising committee. But their heavy-handed zeal, crash-landing it on the house, ruining a football game and disrupting TV reception, antagonizes the townspeople. Herm hires a P.R. man and gets a new image, growing a beard and wearing a snazzy uniform as "Commander" of International Gospel Blimps Inc. Soon consumer groups and big business are adding their messages onto the blimp. Finally, for all Herm's lavish three-year campaign, what saves George's neighbors is the example he and his wife show simply by getting to know them. Joe Bayly's satirical parable, written in 1960 and filmed in 1961, still has a lot to say about evangelical America today.

THE GOSPEL BLIMP, 1974, PUBLISHED BY & © SPIRE CHRISTIAN COMICS/
FLEMING H. REVELL COMPANY, OLD TAPPAN, NEW JERSEY, 32-PAGE COMIC.
WRITTEN AND DRAWN BY AL HARTLEY FROM THE BOOK BY & © JOSEPH P. BAYLY

YOU WANT MORE?   CHRISTIANITY 112   AIRCRAFT 58   UP IN SMOKE

SPIRE CHRISTIAN COMICS
The Gospel Blimp
39¢
ALL HAVE SINNED
DON'T BE A LITTERBUG
Al Hartley

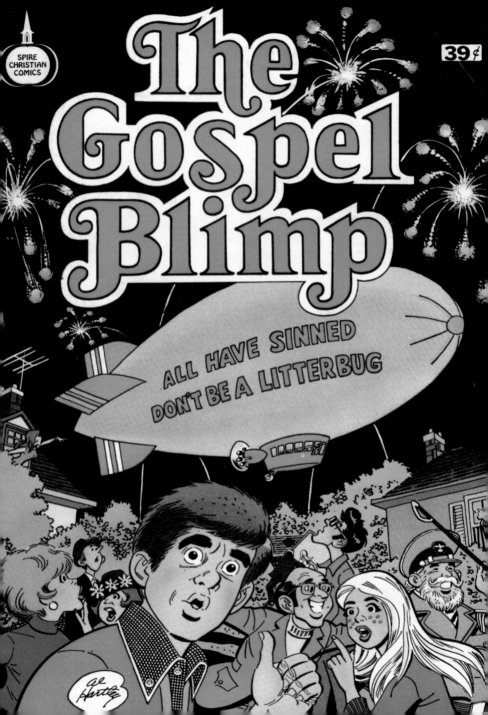

"FEELING GUILTY? NEED TO CONFESS? LET THE LEATHER NUN HELP YOU GET IT OFF YOUR CHEST."

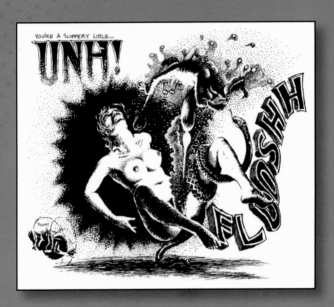

Drug trips, Catholic guilt, Viet Nam war paranoia and S&M and phallic fantasies combine in this blasphemous, heady cocktail. The book opens in a rogue monastery in the Himalayas, where the Leather Nun and her minions unlock the secrets of the Vatican's last scroll, a pagan shaman's forbidden key to negative inner space. They use this to dispatch a captured meek-and-mild agent of the Pope on a demonic form of basic training. Stripped naked, his first tour of duty is an orgy, in which the priapic monsignor climaxes on-stage with the Nun herself. In another tale, the Nun takes a break from punishing the devout by mounting a life-size crucifix, which she can turn on at the flip of a switch. She excuses her outrageous conduct by explaining, "It's OK, we're married."

TALES FROM THE LEATHER NUN NO. 1, SEPTEMBER 1973, LAST GASP ECO-FUNNIES, BERKELEY, CALIFORNIA, 44-PAGE B/W COMIC. COVER BY & © DAVE SHERIDAN, STORIES BY & © DAVE SHERIDAN (ABOVE), ROBERT CRUMB, SPAIN, JAXON, PAT RYAN AND ROGER BRAND

YOU WANT MORE?   NUNS 32   ORGIES 82   LEATHER 36

TALES FROM THE
LEATHER NUN
OVS
LAST GASP
$1.50
ADU
ONLY

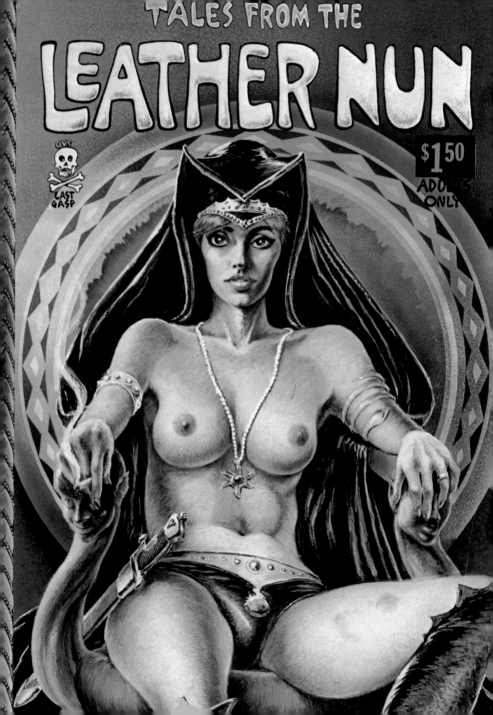

"GEE, DAD, I HAD NO IDEA WHAT WAS BEHIND KHRUSHCHEV'S SHOE POUNDING."

TWO FACES OF COMMUNISM

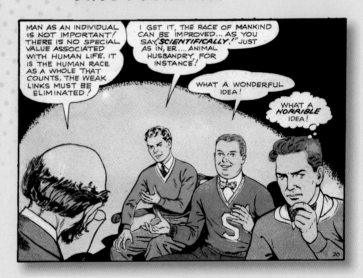

With a shiny halo overhead, Nikita Khrushchev smiles over the fence and invites us to "leave the stupid capitalist side and enjoy the glories of OUR paradise." But turn the page and you see that behind the fence the true communist garden is filled with a vegetable patch of missiles, a bed of skull-shaped flowers and a big sack of "seeds for godlessness." We then join the Jacksons in Your Town, U.S.A., as Dad tells the kids about the threat of communism. Dad knows so much about it because while at university one of his professors was secretly a commie agent who almost managed to convert him to the communist cause. Luckily, his "sincere belief in God" leads him to reject their doctrines and get the Red "quietly removed from his position and turned over to the F.B.I." This Cold War comic was part of the Christian Anti-Communist Crusade's array of propaganda, including booklets sold as "midget missiles" and "penny projectiles."

TWO FACES OF COMMUNISM, 1961, PUBLISHED BY & © THE CHRISTIAN ANTI-COMMUNIST CRUSADE, HOUSTON, TEXAS, 36-PAGE COMIC. PRODUCED BY FEATURE PUBLICATIONS, INC., NEW YORK AND DRAWN BY PETE COSTANZA.

YOU WANT MORE?   COMMIES 110   WORLD LEADERS 64   CHRISTIANITY 112

Two Faces

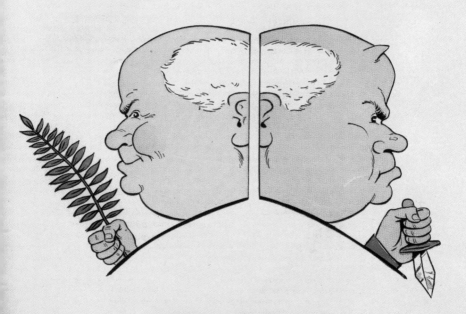

OF

COMMUNISM

"THE GO-GO WONDER OF PARIS -- THAT'S SPACE GIRL. TRANSISTORS NEVER WEAR DOWN. THEY JUST GO ON AND ON -- EVEN HER HEART IS MADE OF VINYL."

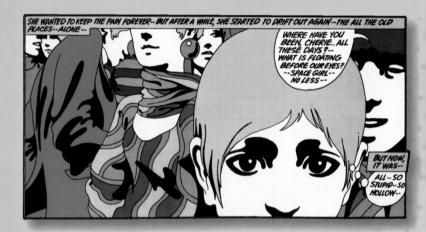

In this Swinging Sixties threesome of related romances, Pam is hopelessly in love with penniless Olly from the mod group The Cleets, whose big chance comes when they open at The Poo, "the innest of the outest discos in all London," but Pam has a rival for Olly's affections in his former French lover, Nicole. Next, the improbably named Londoner Loom Prescott joins his friend Tony in a taxi cab chasing across Italy after the girl they both fancy. Finally, we make the scene with Space Girl, "The Hippest Girl in the World," an American actress looking for love but not marriage in Paris, "half teenybopper, half vampire, her orbit starts at sundown." This upscale 50-cent magazine with card cover and glossy pages comes in eye-poppingly psychedelic colors.

MOD LOVE NO. 1, 1967, PUBLISHED BY & © WESTERN PUBLISHING COMPANY, INC., POUGHKEEPSIE, NEW YORK, 36-PAGE MAGAZINE. WRITTEN BY MICHAEL LUTIN, ILLUSTRATOR UNCREDITED

YOU WANT MORE?   ROMANCE 120   POP MUSIC 44   LONDON 106

50
MOD LOVE
• SHADOW FROM HIS PAST
• AS LONG AS I WIN
HE'S THE HIPPEST GIRL IN THE WORLD

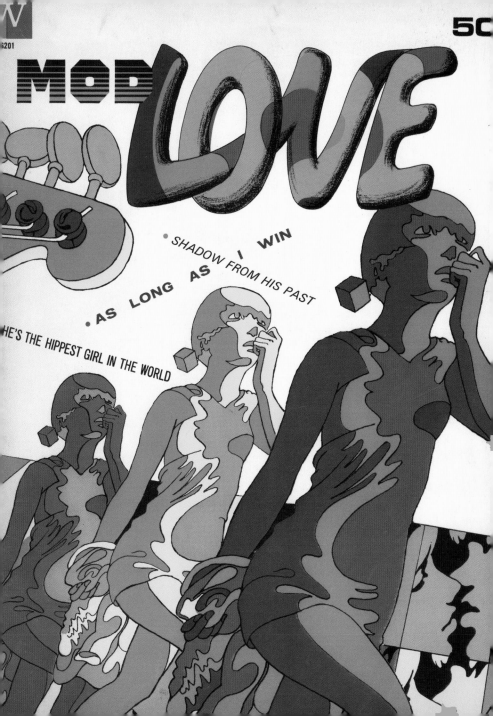

"HOT TEMPERS AND HOT-RODS ARE OUT!"

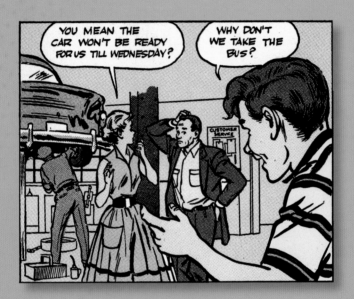

"Where did YOU learn to drive?" Cutting in line, ranting at other drivers for lane-dodging, his road-raging Dad doesn't present young Tommy with the most positive role model. On the way to the lake, they have trouble with the car and stop at a garage. At the nearby bus station, Tommy gets talking with a Greyhound driver, who takes him through all the "safety savvy" he's been trained in, tips which "you can adapt to personal motoring." By the end, with their automobile out of action, his parents jump at Tommy's idea of taking the bus instead. Reclining in his seat, Dad dozes off while Tommy fantasizes, "Wouldn't it be keen to drive a bus like this, Dad?" Despite all its advice for motorists, the real message to them is: "Go Greyhound, and leave the driving to us!"

DRIVING LIKE A PRO, 1958, PUBLISHED BY & © THE GREYHOUND CORPORATION, CHICAGO, 16-PAGE FREE COMIC. WRITER AND ARTIST UNCREDITED

YOU WANT MORE?   DEAR DADS 92   ON THE ROAD 76   CAREERS 80

DRIVING LIKE A PRO
Relax

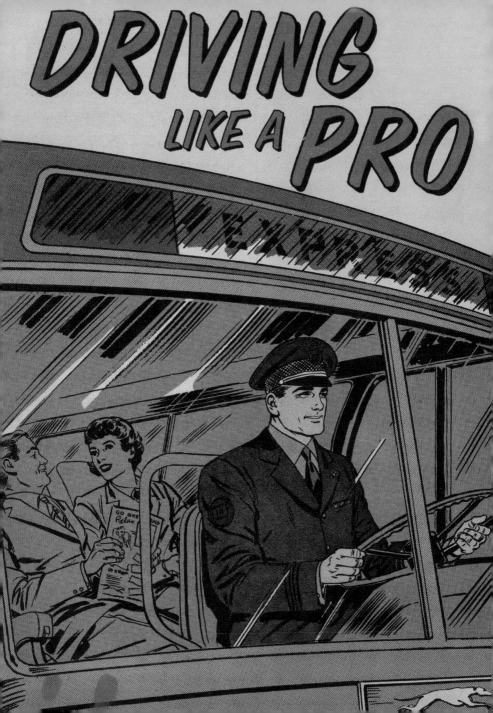

"HOPEFULLY, THIS BOOK HELPS TO GUIDE YOUR EVERYDAY DEEDS."

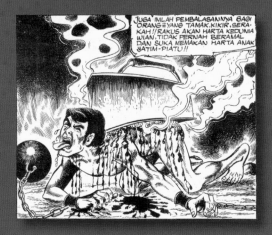

Here's one way to get your kids to behave. According to its fervent Malay author, this comic is intended to "teach young children a good way of life." One look through page after page of the naked and the damned subjected to the goriest ordeals outside of Catholic visions of purgatory or torture-porn movies ought to completely traumatize them into being perfect little darlings. Two cloaked messengers from God take the Prophet Muhammad, represented only as a circle containing his name in traditional Thuluth calligraphy, on a guided tour of the fiery pits of Neraka (hell) to see how the punishment varies to fit the crime. Some sinners have their tongues or limbs cut off, stakes and pincers applied to their genitals or boiling water poured over their heads. Others endure a giant steam iron searing the flesh off their back, all shown in nauseating detail. And worst of all, their wounds heal, so their suffering can resume for eternity. Mr. Jaya states proudly that "some of the contents were taken from the Qur'an and Hadith, but the illustrations were all done from the artist's imagination." It makes Dante's *Inferno* look like a wet weekend.

NERAKA, UNDATED, POSSIBLY 1980S, PUBLISHED IN MALAYSIA, NO PUBLISHER DETAILS, 36-PAGE SMALL B/W COMIC. PRODUCED BY M.A. JAYA, ILLUSTRATED BY "YUN"

NERAK
ILL: YUN

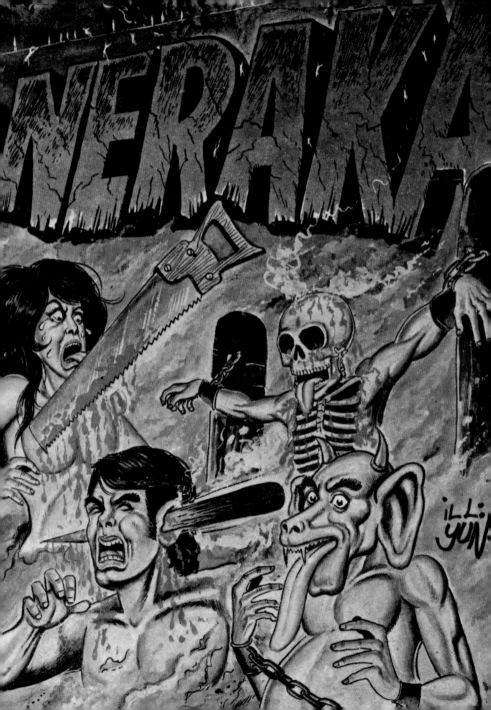

"WHY ARE YOU SNIFFING LIKE THAT, PETER?"

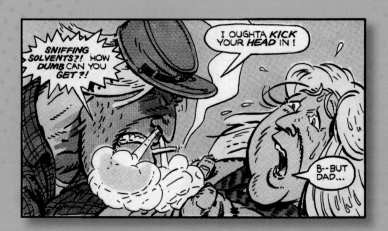

One night, mild-mannered Inuk Peter wakes to find that he has been chosen to receive a five-toothed charm which confers on him the power to become Super Shamou, protector of the people of the Arctic. The first Inuit superhero—with rubber boots and a receding hairline—originated as a live-action TV character played by co-creator Peter Tapatai in three educational films from the Inuit Broadcasting Corporation. Tapatai was also the model for the comic version, state-funded and double-covered, in English and Inuit. Youngsters, bored during long winter nights in isolated communities, turn to glue-sniffing, which puts them and their pals in danger. Super Shamou rescues kids from a fire caused by their habit, and another from drowning in an icy lake, but he realizes the community has come to rely on him always to save them. So he motivates them to work together to solve the bigger problem for themselves and then slips away unnoticed to resume his civilian identity—for now.

SUPER SHAMOU NO. 1, 1987, PUBLISHED BY & © THE INUIT BROADCASTING CORPORATION, OTTAWA, ONTARIO, CANADA, 36-PAGE COMIC. CREATED BY BARNEY PATTUNGUYAK AND PETER TAPATAI, WRITTEN AND DRAWN BY NICK BURNS.

YOU WANT MORE?   PROBLEM KIDS 16   FROZEN NORTH 62   MAGIC 12

#1
IT BROADCASTING
CORPORATION
SUPER SHAMOU
NOTHING TO SNIFF AT!

"SUDDENLY, I FEEL UNCOMFORTABLE HAVING THE ROSARY SO NEAR TO MY...UH...TROUSERS!"

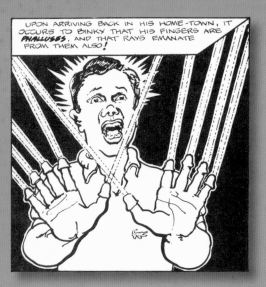

Could you survive an adolescence tormented by the fear that your "pecker rays" might intersect with a Church and damn you as "one of Satan's agents?" Nobody before Justin Green had dared to confess their most private sacrilegious and psychosexual fixations so candidly in comics. Through his alter ego Binky Brown, Green re-enacts the escalating traumas of his youth, rooted in repressive schooling by "fascistic" nuns and in behaviour that would now be treated as obsessive compulsive disorder. Steeped from an early age in strict Catholic dogma, he struggles to apply it rigorously to every aspect of his life. To stay "pure" and rid himself of "homo thoughts about Christ," his penances include banging his head repeatedly on the headboard of his bed. But his overactive guilt imagines more phalluses on his fingers, feet, footprints, even ordinary objects, whose sinful beams drive him to elaborate rituals to compensate. Only as an adult does Binky find some catharsis when he buys and smashes a dozen Madonnas, saving the one which survives unscathed. Green's "must reading for neurotics of every creed" inspired the whole confessional comics movement.

BINKY BROWN MEETS THE HOLY VIRGIN MARY, 1972, PUBLISHED BY LAST GASP ECO-FUNNIES, BERKELEY, CALIFORNIA, 44-PAGE B/W COMIC. WRITTEN AND DRAWN BY & © JUSTIN GREEN

YOU WANT MORE?   NUNS 20   SIN 28   MADNESS 100

BINKY BROWN
50¢
YOUNGSTERS PROHIBITED
meets The Holy
Virgin Mary
SPEAK, MY SON.
BUT– MY THOUGHTS
NO!
IMPURE THOUGHTS
NO!

"EVEN IF I EAT KASCO EGG PRODUCER A HUNDRED TIMES A DAY I COULDN'T LAY ONE THAT SIZE!"

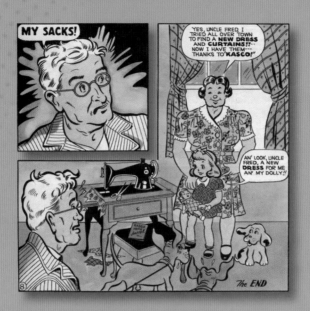

The same year that Toledo-based cartoonist Bill Woggon created the "Pin-Up Queen" Katy Keene for Archie Comics, he also came up with another "KK," the less fashion-crazy farm girl Kitty Kasco. In plaid shirt and overalls she promotes the virtues of Kasco Feed with Uncle Fred. It's another fun schoolday at Kitty's Kindergarten as she teaches her chick pupils about the 17 common diseases they are susceptible to, from omphalitis to gape worms, and the cleansing properties of Kasco Flushing Mash. Meanwhile, Uncle Fred frets over his missing empty feed bags, until he discovers his wife Martha has recycled the floral-print sacks into curtains and new dresses for herself, their niece and her little dolly. This nibbled copy came stamped on the back by the Tittsworth Bros. store in Ellicott City, Maryland who first gave it away.

KASCO COMICS NO. 1, 1945, PUBLISHED BY & © KASCO MILLS, INC., TOLEDO, OHIO, 28-PAGE FREE COMIC.
WRITTEN AND DRAWN BY BILL WOGGON

KASCO
KOMICS
KASCO
28 PAGES OF FUN FOR THE FAMILY!!
featuring
KITTY KASCO • UNCLE FRED
plus
GAMES • PUZZLES • TRICKS
FARM ODDITIES • HILARIOUS GAGS
BILL WOGGON

SWEETER GWEN

"WHAT LUCK! MY BODY JUST CRAVES A GOOD WORKOUT!"

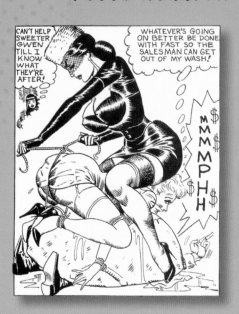

In the pre-internet, pre-video days, if you had a private predilection for images of "bondage, girl-fighting and similar bizarre subjects," your prime source, apart perhaps from a copy of *Wonder Woman* or *Sheena*, used to be mail-order outfits like Irving Klaw's in New York. Klaw would sell you photographic prints of fetish comics, tame by today's standards, and they didn't come cheap; the first three pages of *Sweeter Gwen* would set you back $5 each, or $12 for the three in August 1962, when a whole comic book still cost ten cents. Still, aficionados would pay whatever it cost for extremely tight dresses and ropes, high heels, plunging necklines and girl-on-girl action. In *Sweeter Gwen* Eric Stanton pays tribute to *Sweet Gwendoline*, Singapore-born Englishman John Willie's melodramatic serial which defined the kinky genre. Foul fiends D'Astard D'Astardly and the Mysterious Countess truss up Gwen again to locate a secret map to a mine. Only when Gwen bestrides D'Astardly does he look up and notice that the birthmark on her left buttock is "a tiny roadmap". Gwen is saved by buxom YU-69 after a savage cat-fight with the Countess, but her map is lost when D'Astardly accidentally brands her behind. The inking style stirred false rumors that Stanton was secretly Steve Ditko, but for at least ten years they did share a studio.

SWEETER GWEN, 1976, PUBLISHED BY BÉLIER PRESS, INC., NEW YORK, 60-PAGE B/W COMIC MAGAZINE. WRITTEN AND DRAWN BY & © ERIC STANTON

BONUS! GIANT FULL-COLOR POSTER INSIDE!!
Stanton Presents
SWEETER GWEN & the RETURN of GWENDOLINE
2 CLASSIC CARTOON ADVENTURE SERIALS

"STRANGE, I DON'T WATCH MUCH FOOTBALL, BUT THAT OWN GOAL LOOKED ALMOST DELIBERATE!"

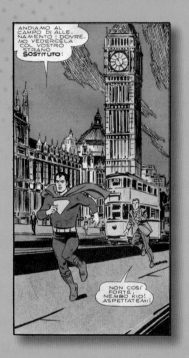

Who's that zooming over the World Cup football pitch in London in 1966? Yes, it's Superman, but in his Italian guise as Nembo Kid (*nembo* being the Italian word for the cloud type nimbus). Publishers Mondadori dropped the Superman name in 1954, perhaps worried that the name might remind readers of Nietzsche's *übermensch* philosophy, which was incorrectly associated with Nazism. This meant having to blank out the "S" symbol on his chest and replace the word "super" with "ultra" to describe his powers. In the Sixties Mondadori had Italian creators devise new stories to fill the weekly title. Under pressure from the moral guardians Garanzia Morale, Italy's Comics Code, they cut back on the fantasy aspects. In "The Big Scam" Nembo Kid is often less powerful, weakened by kryptonite, and, more realistically, hardly flies at all. Instead, he jogs to the rescue, as shown above; he might have arrived quicker by taking the tram (except that trams disappeared from London in 1952). His journalist alter ego Clark Kent plays a bigger role and uncovers an illegal gambling den, kidnapping top players and somehow planting identical substitutes to play poorly and fix matches. It's a topical story, issued within days of the World Cup kicking off in London.

NEMBO KID NO. 535, JULY 17, 1966, PUBLISHED BY ARNOLDO MONDADORI EDITORE, MILAN, ITALY, 100-PAGE DIGEST. SUPERMAN ™ & © 2008 DC COMICS. COVER BY ANTONIO TOLDO & ENRICO BAGNOLI, WRITTEN BY PIER CARPI OR ROBERTO CATALANO, AND DRAWN BY RAFFAELE PAPARELLA

YOU WANT MORE?   SPORTS 118   LONDON 24   SUPERHEROES 126

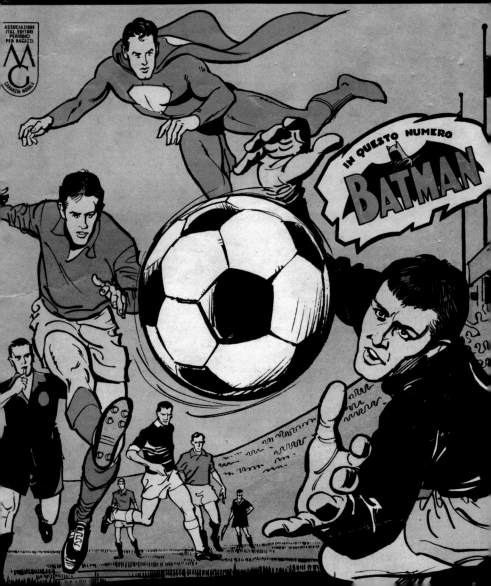

NEMBO KID

N. 535   Pubblicazione settimanale   17 luglio 1966   100 PAGINE

ASSOCIAZIONE
ITAL. EDITORI
PERIODICI
PER RAGAZZI

M G

GARANZIA MORALE

IN QUESTO NUMERO

BATMAN

"HE'S HERE! AH DONE FOUND HIM! GATHER UP YORE HORNS, AXES, MISERY STICKS, MEN! WE-ALL GONNA HAVE OURSELVES A BALL!"

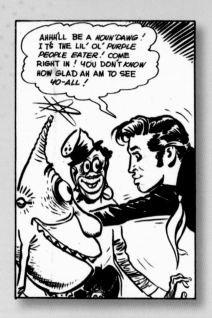

Within months of the Sheb Wooley No.1 novelty hit in June 1958 came this Australian oddity revealing the full story of how the one-eyed, one-horned alien Pirpo's love of rock'n'roll makes him lose his appetite for purple people and gets him banished to Earth, where he wants to join a band. Here Pirpo meets: the racist caricature of the distinguished witchdoctor, Livingstone Ah Presoom Zombi, who becomes his manager; an English aristocrat in the Terry-Thomas mould, Ffoull-Featherstone, whose haunted castle Pirpo flattens when the ghosts dig his crazy rhythms; and gloomy Elvis parody Nervus Purvis, who is reinvigorated by Pirpo's music and helps make him a superstar via his TV show. Finally, Pirpo returns to his purple home planet where the Purple People are no longer being eaten, but are now "rock'n'rollin' with the Purple People Eaters!" Thirty years later a movie would be made about Pirpo, but Trowell's "hep" 1958 comic got there first.

THE PURPLE PEOPLE EATER, SEPTEMBER 1958, PUBLISHED BY & © MODERN MAGAZINES PTY. LTD., SYDNEY, AUSTRALIA, 32-PAGE COMIC, B/W WITH FOUR INTERIOR PAGES IN COLOR. WRITTEN AND DRAWN BY TERRY TROWELL

YOU WANT MORE?   POP MUSIC 84   ALIENS 98   TELEVISION 12

No! No! not the... PURPLE PEOPLE EATER

TERRY TROWELL

"DIDN'T YOU EVER WONDER WHY HE WALKED FUNNY?"

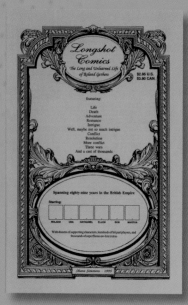

Here's proof that you should never let an almost total lack of drawing ability deter you from making comics. Canadian writer Shane Simmons' inspired solution is to draw his entire cast so far away that they look like black dots in the far distance. Taking minimalism to new heights, he used 3,840 tiny square panels to tell the blackly humorous saga of "The Long and Unlearned Life of Roland Gethers." With sharp dialogue and comic timing worthy of *Monty Python's Flying Circus*, he unfolds the faltering fortunes of this Welsh miner's 12th son, from his tragic childbirth in 1860, which ends his mother's life, through school, marriage, war, and illness to the end of his days. Incredibly, this epic in miniature—spanning 89 years of the British Empire—makes us care about these inky specs on paper. Originally self-published through the aptly named Eyestrain Productions as a photocopied 80-page mini-comic in 1993, it was reissued in regular American comic size in 1995. A sequel, "The Failed Promise of Bradley Gethers," appeared in 1997.

LONGSHOT COMICS NO. 1, 1995, SLAVE LABOR GRAPHICS PUBLISHING, SAN JOSE, CALIFORNIA, 28-PAGE B/W COMIC. WRITTEN AND "DRAWN" BY & © SHANE SIMMONS

CARDIFF, WALES 1860
DOCTOR! THANK GOODNESS YOU'VE COME.
IT'S MARTHA, SHE'S IN AN AWFUL WAY.
WHAT'S THE TROUBLE?
WELL, SHE'S WITH CHILD...
AGAIN? OH, YOU CATHOLICS.
HOW MANY DOES THAT MAKE?
AH...I CAN'T REMEMBER RIGHT NOW.
BUT LOOK, MARTHA'S JUST UPSTAIRS.
IT'S NEVER BEEN LIKE THIS BEFORE.
I'D BETTER GO SEE HER THEN.
UPSTAIRS
HELLO MARTHA.
AND HOW ARE WE THIS EVENING?
ARRG! OOOOG! YAARRRRR!
THAT BAD, HMMM?
OH DOCTOR! THE PAIN! IT'S AGONY!
THERE THERE.
IT'S ALL PART OF BIRTHING.
TRY NOT TO DWELL ON IT.
DWELL ON IT?
SORRY, BUT IT'S A LITTLE PREOCCUPYING
...HAVING A SMALL HUMAN BEING TRYING TO CLAW ITS WAY OUT OF YOUR PRIVATES!
NOW NOW MRS. GETHERS, IT'S NOT AS BAD AS ALL THAT.
ERRRG!
HOW WOULD YOU KNOW YOU BLOODY GREAT PONCE!
PASS ANY CITRUS FRUIT-SIZED TURDS ON THE POT LATELY?
MRS. GETHERS, PLEASE.
THAT'S JUST THE PAIN TALKING.
YES! AND I'M IN RATHER A LOT OF IT RIGHT NOW!
WHY DON'T YOU GIVE ME SOMETHING FOR IT INSTEAD OF MAKING SMALL TALK?
ALL RIGHT. HANG ON.
I'LL GIVE YOU A SHOT OF MORPHINE.
MAKE IT A DOUBLE.
YOU WOMEN DO GO ON WHEN YOU'RE IN LABOUR.
I'VE DELIVERED OVER A HUNDRED BABIES...
AND EVERY DELIVERY HAS GONE SMOOTHLY AND EASILY IN THE END.
EXCEPT FOR THE ONES IN WHICH THE MOTHER OR THE BABY OR BOTH DIED.
BUT THE REST...
IT'S THE MOST NATURAL THING THERE IS.
AND JUST ABOUT THE MOST PAINFUL! OOORRRF!
DON'T EXAGGERATE.
OH? AND HOW MANY CHILDREN HAVE YOU PERSONALLY GIVEN BIRTH TO, DOCTOR?
WELL... NONE.
BUT I'VE DELIVERED...
DELIVERED! HA!
ME, I'VE HAD...
UM...
WELL I CAN'T QUITE REMEMBER HOW MANY I'VE HAD JUST AT THE MOMENT...
BUT I'VE HAD A LOT!
AND THEY ALL HURT LIKE A BUGGER!
THIS ONE'S THE WORST.
WELL I DON'T UNDERSTAND THAT.
CHILDBIRTH SHOULD GET EASIER THE MORE... OH DEAR.
WHAT?
I MUST HAVE LEFT THE MORPHINE IN MY OTHER BAG.
AAAAAGG!
SURELY YOU MUST HAVE SOMETHING!
UM... OH HERE. JUST THE THING.
I'VE GOT A BULLET.
BITE ON THIS.
ERR-CHOMP
THERE. THAT BETTER?
NNNNNNGGG
I'LL TAKE THAT AS A "YES".
ALL RIGHT NOW, MARTHA. PUSH!
NNNNNNGGG!
PUSH! PUSH HARD!
NNNNNNGGG!
AGAIN!
NNNNNNGGG! KA-POW
DON'T BITE THE BULLET QUITE THAT HARD MRS. GETHERS.
OWOWOW! I THING I BURN'D M' TONG!
NEVER MIND THAT NOW.
YOUR AIM WAS OFF ANYWAY.
YAAAARG!
I CAN SEE THE HEAD!
PUSH MARTHA! KEEP PUSHING!
EIIIIIIIGG!
PUSH!
EIIII
HERE IT COMES!
GOT IT!
SWAT
WAAAAAA!
VERY GOOD, MRS. GETHERS.
ANOTHER FINE YOUNG STRAPPING BOY.
MRS. GETHERS?
OH DEAR.
DOWN AT THE PUB
SO WHAT HAVE YOU NAMED YOUR NEW SON?
NAMES? I'VE NO TIME FOR NAMES.
THERE'S TOO MUCH TO DO 'ROUND THE HOUSE SINCE MARTHA'S PASSING.
SURELY YOU'LL TAKE THE BOY TO BE BAPTIZED.
YOU HAVE TO GIVE HIM A PROPER CHRISTIAN NAME.
IT'LL BE DONE WHEN I GET TO IT.
TILL THEN, "THE BABY" WILL DO.
HE'S JUST A TINY LITTLE THING...
AND NO ONE WILL MISTAKE WHO WE'RE TALKING ABOUT.
HE MAKES TWELVE DOESN'T HE?
AYE. TWELVE FINE CHILDREN AND BOYS EVERY ONE.
YOU'VE BEEN TRULY BLESSED.
I SUPPOSE.
BUT I CAN'T HELP BUT WISH MARTHA HAD GIVEN ME ONE DAUGHTER.
AND NOW SHE'S GONE, LEAVING A HOUSE FULL OF MEN.
NEVER A DAUGHTER WILL I HAVE.
AND WHO, WHO I ASK YOU, WILL DO THE LAUNDRY?
I CAN FEEL YOUR GRIEF.
AYE. 'TIS A TRAGIC TIME FOR US ALL.
LIFE AT HOME
WAAAAAAA!
JOSHUA! SAMUEL! DANIEL!
YES FATHER?
WHY'S THE BABY CRYING NOW?
HE MUST BE HUNGRY.
OR DIRTY.
OR ILL.
WELL WHAT IS IT THEN?
A HUNGRY, DIRTY, OR ILL CRY?
I DON'T KNOW.
ME NEITHER.
NOR I.
WHAT ARE WE SUPPOSED TO DO TO GET HIM TO STOP?
WE COULD FEED HIM.
OR CHANGE HIM.
OR NURSE HIM BACK TO HEALTH.
HRM. RIGHT.
TRY SOME OF THAT THEN.
SEE IF IT DOESN'T SHUT HIM UP FOR A BIT.
YES FATHER.
WAAAAAAA!
WAAAAAAA!
WAAAAAAA!
BLAST IT!
JOSHUA! SAMUEL! DANIEL!
YES FATHER?
THE BABY IS STILL CRYING.
YES FATHER.
DIDN'T YOU TRY TO PUT A STOP TO IT?
YES, BUT THE BABY ISN'T HUNGRY OR DIRTY OR ILL.
WELL WHAT THE BLOODY HELL IS IT THEN?
THE BABY'S TEETHING, FATHER.
OH.
SO WHAT DO WE DO FOR THAT ONE?
ER... NOTHING FATHER.
JUST LET IT HAPPEN, I SUPPOSE.
WELL HOW LONG IS THIS GOING TO GO ON FOR?
I DON'T KNOW, FATHER.
MORE THAN FIVE MINUTES?
I THINK SO, FATHER.
BLAST! I CAN'T HEAR MYSELF THINK IN HERE.
WELL WHAT DID YOU DO WHEN WE WERE TEETHING FATHER?
LET YOUR MOTHER TAKE CARE OF YOU WHILE I POPPED DOWN THE PUB FOR A PINT.
OH.
CAN'T CALL ON YOUR MOTHER ANYMORE.
NO.
'COURSE I CAN STILL POP DOWN THE PUB FOR A PINT.

"DYNOMITE! WILLIE, I COULD KISS THAT FAT ON YOUR HEAD!"

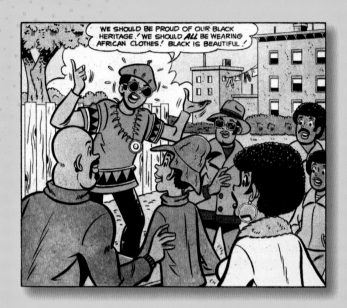

Hailing from MoCity, as in Motown, the suggestively named Fast Willie has the funky flares, Afro hair and street talk of Michael's secret missing Jackson brother. The way Willie and his "cool, bad, fast, and together brothers and sisters" look and act also suggests that they are related to Archie and the Riverdale gang, and in fact artist Gus Lemoine drew for Archie Comics. Frustrated at their reluctance in the early 1970s to add more than token ethnic characters to their white cast, Lemoine joined forces with black entrepreneur Bert Fitzgerald to create an all-African-American Archie. They combined Betty and Veronica into one love interest, delectable Dee Dee, and gave Willie two rivals for her, sugar daddy Frankie Johnson and rabid militant Jabar. Despite their "positive discrimination," the racial stereotypes were broad and the only "honky" regular was hapless Officer Flagg, or "The Man." Still, a survey found that kids both black and white were "digging it," though not enough for it to last more than seven issues.

FAST WILLIE JACKSON NO. 1, OCTOBER 1976, PUBLISHED BY & © FITZGERALD PERIODICALS, NEW YORK, 36-PAGE COMIC. CREATED BY BERT FITZGERALD AND GUS LEMOINE

YOU WANT MORE?   AFRICAN-AMERICANS 50 POP MUSIC 44 FASHIONS 52

CAN YOU DIG IT?
YEAH! I CAN DIG IT!
FAST WILLIE JACKSON
30¢
PDC
53160-9
G. LEMOINE

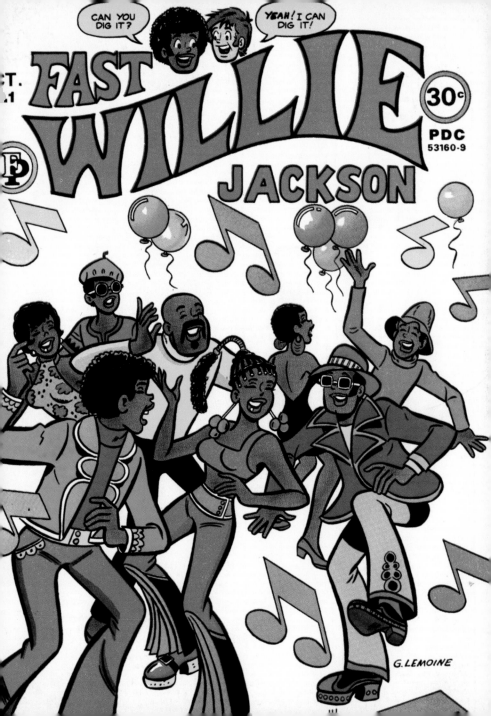

"NEVER HAD SHE SIGHTED ONE SO DASHING, SO MAGNETIC, SO GAY... SO CLEAN!"

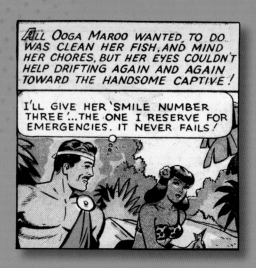

ALL OOGA MAROO WANTED TO DO WAS CLEAN HER FISH, AND MIND HER CHORES, BUT HER EYES COULDN'T HELP DRIFTING AGAIN AND AGAIN TOWARD THE HANDSOME CAPTIVE!

I'LL GIVE HER 'SMILE NUMBER THREE'...THE ONE I RESERVE FOR EMERGENCIES. IT NEVER FAILS!

JON JUAN

The father of American superheroes, Jerry Siegel, leaps from writing celibate *Superman*, always fending off Lois Lane's advances, to Super-Lover Jon Juan, the "irresistible lover, slavishly adored by the most fascinating women of all time." Jon's reputation for stealing hearts goes back to his origins in ancient Atlantis. Here, a disgruntled husband and champion discus-hurler gives "that love-struck gallant a love-tap on his wily noggin!" Knocked unconscious, preserved in an iceberg, Jon Juan thaws out to find that a rare seaweed has made him immortal. So now the eternal lover can seduce every woman he meets, from his first rescuer, cavegirl Ooga Maroo in her leopard-skin bikini, to a blind señorita and a sleeping beauty in Baghdad. There's a hint of melancholy, however, as the confirmed bachelor reminisces alone in his remote Tibetan palace about all the beauties he has left behind, gazing at the trophies in his "secret archives of love." His dashing smile and moustache suggest that Jon Juan may have been modeled partly on Errol Flynn and Clark Gable, and perhaps on a young Douglas Fairbanks, who at 51 played the role of an ageing Don Juan in his final picture in 1934.

JON JUAN, SPRING 1950, PUBLISHED BY & © TOBY PRESS, NEW YORK, 36-PAGE COMIC. WRITTEN BY JERRY SIEGEL AND DRAWN BY ALEX SCHOMBURG UNDER THE PEN-NAME AL REID

YOU WANT MORE?   ROMANCE 102   GORGEOUSNESS 120   HOLLYWOOD 6

HE ONE AND ONLY SUPERLOVER!!
JON JUAN
ANC
BY
JERRY SIEGEL
ORIGINATOR OF
SUPERMAN
10¢
NO.1
HE FIGHTS!
HE LOVES!
HE DARES!

"THE LOW-DOWN, BONE-PICKIN', SNAKE-EATIN' SON OF A MANGEY CAYOTE!"

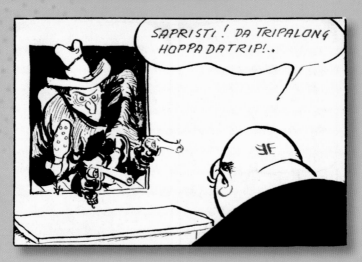

Emile Mercier, born in 1901, the son of a French baker on the Pacific islands of New Caledonia, first flourished in one-shot comics in the Forties, many of them zany pastiches of popular American heroes, such as Supa Dupa Man and Mudrake the Magician. In Tripalong Hoppity Mercier parodies Hopalong Cassidy, Clarence E. Mulford's rough'n'ready wrangler, whom actor William Boyd cleaned up to play in 66 movies from 1935. In the arid Texas desert, Tripalong takes on cruel cattle baron El Stingo, who is menacing his pal Gaspar and his secret underground creek, which provides water, fish and pansies and runs a "gimerator" supplying lighting and electricity: "Guess I'm fur ahead of that hombre Edison." Reaching Stingo's ranch on his trusty steed Tinplate, Tripalong sneaks up to his quarters by squeezing into the service lift, and then frees his captive, a traveling salesman. In the final showdown, when the bullets run out, the fearless Texas Ranger sets off the salesman's samples— fireworks—which soon have the villains on the run.

TRIPALONG HOPPITY, 1944, PUBLISHED BY FRANK JOHNSON, SYDNEY, AUSTRALIA, 36-PAGE B/W COMIC. WRITTEN AND DRAWN BY & © EMILE MERCIER

TRIPALONG HOPPITY
The Fearless TEXAS RANGER
6D
By EMILE MERCIER
A FRANK JOHNSON PRODUCTION

"THAT LI'L DEVIL WILL BE THE DEATH OF ME YET."

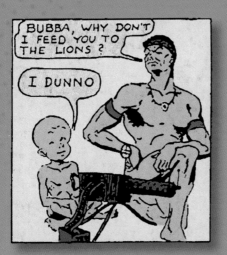

Back in the Forties, black people were underrepresented in American comics and typically played supporting characters, menials, comedy relief or naïve natives. Born in 1902, Orrin C. Evans grew up with the effects of racism. By passing for white, his light-skinned father had secured a far better job than a black man was usually allowed, but to keep up appearances when work colleagues dropped round, he hid his darker-skinned son in a back room. Evans became a reporter and was the first black journalist hired by a major white paper, the *Philadelphia Record*. When that paper closed, Evans formed a partnership, including two *Record* editors, to launch the first comic in which blacks play all the lead roles and "every brush stroke and pen line...are by Negro artists." Evans and younger brother George invent the first black hero in comic books, Lion Man (above). "American-born, college educated," he is sent to Africa "by the United Nations to watch over...the world's largest deposit of uranium—enough to make an atom bomb that could destroy the world." Lion Man foils Dr. Brut Sangro's plan to steal the ore, but when his pesky Zulu orphan sidekick Bubba tries to help by machine-gunning Sangro's accomplice, the evil doctor sneaks away. The comic's other stars also grace the cover: police detective Ace Harlem; the cute Dew Dillies with mermaid Bubbles and angel Bibber; and jive-talking Sugarfoot and Snake-Oil. A second issue was ready to roll, but was abandoned when all suppliers suspiciously refused to sell Evans more newsprint. It still stands, as he wrote in his editorial, as a "milestone in the splendid history of Negro journalism."

ALL-NEGRO COMICS NO. 1, JUNE 1947, PUBLISHED BY & © ALL-NEGRO COMICS, INC., PHILADELPHIA, 52-PAGE COMIC. COVER BY BILL DRISCOLL, INTERIORS BY ORRIN C. EVANS AND VARIOUS ARTISTS

YOU WANT MORE?   ATOMIC 8   AFRICAN-AMERICANS 44   AFRICA 112

COMICS PUBLICATION
ALL-NEGRO COMICS
15¢

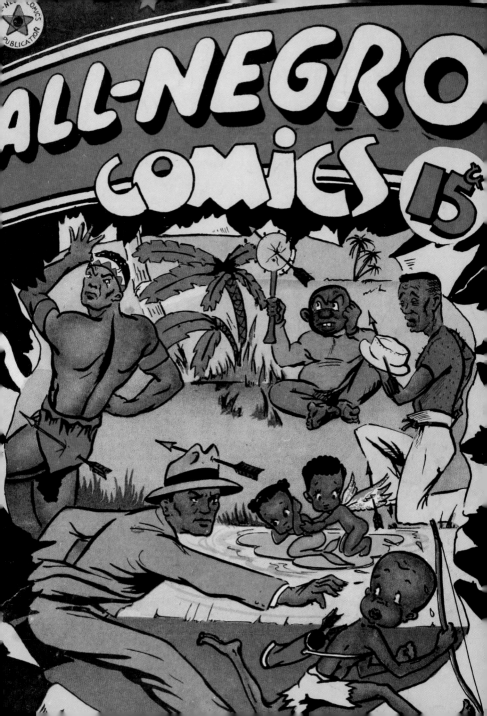

"MAN, I TELL IT LIKE IT IS NOW! THE SOUND IS GROOVEY! IT BLOWS MY MIND!"

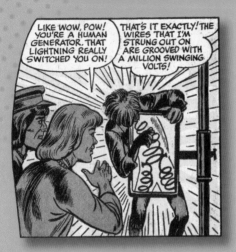

Joe Simon, co-creator of Captain America and 55 at the time, originally wanted to call his "ultimate hippie" the Freak, but this was vetoed by the conservative publishers so he was renamed the Geek. In "A Thing is Born," Hell's Angel Hound Dawg and the Mongrels are harassing the peace-loving hippies in a former tailor's workshop. To stop their wet clothes shrinking, the hippies put some on an old dummy and forget it for months, until a lightning bolt brings it to life. The flower-power champion smashes the biker gang, learns to speak and play "groovey" guitar, before being kidnapped by the Psychedelic Circus. Breaking free, painted like a doll, the Geek runs for congress, but the Circus, bikers and National Guard conspire and force him to ride his bike off San Francisco's Bay Bridge. Has he gone to a watery grave? "Find out in the next swinging issue!" According to Simon, it was cancelled after the second number, despite healthy sales, because uptight editor Mort Weisinger "claimed it was a subtle drug publication."

BROTHER POWER THE GEEK NO. 1, SEPTEMBER—OCTOBER 1968, PUBLISHED BY NATIONAL PERIODICAL PUBLICATIONS, NEW YORK, 36-PAGE COMIC. ™ & © 2008 DC COMICS. WRITTEN & DRAWN BY JOE SIMON

YOU WANT MORE?   BIKERS 106   BEATNIKS 84   FASHIONS 34

DC NATIONAL COMICS
BROTHER POWER
THE GEEK
APPROVED BY THE COMICS CODE AUTHORITY
OCT.
NO. 1
12¢
A THING THAT LIVES AND FIGHTS FOR ITS SOUL!
HERE IS THE REAL-LIFE SCENE OF THE DANGERS IN HIPPIE-LAND!

"ALL PRUNES ARE PLUMS, BUT NOT ALL PLUMS ARE PRUNES."

A FORTUNE IN TWO OLD TRUNKS

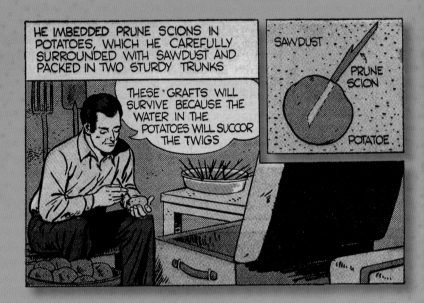

Dark, wrinkly and possessing a laxative effect, prunes don't have the greatest image, so this promotional comic tries to improve matters by revealing the little-known history of how the first prune tree was planted in California in 1856. The gold rush brings brothers Louis and Pierre Pellier over from France in 1848, but when they fail to find gold Pierre heads back home. He later brings over his bride and two trunks filled with scions or shoots of the French "petite prune d'Agen." Grafting them onto root stocks of the native wild plum, the Pelliers establish America's prune industry. Further pages show prunes through history, with fruit-based Bible quotes and the example of Alexander the Great encouraging his troops to eat prunes for breakfast. The comic concludes with farming, drying and packaging methods, health benefits and serving suggestions, for example as a relish for meats or as party snacks "for all occasions."

A FORTUNE IN TWO OLD TRUNKS, 1955, PUBLISHED BY & © THE CALIFORNIA PRUNE AND APRICOT GROWERS ASSOCIATION, SAN JOSÉ, CALIFORNIA, 16-PAGE FREE COMIC. WRITER AND ARTIST UNCREDITED

YOU WANT MORE?   ON THE FARM 60   GOOD ADVICE 14   FOOD 34

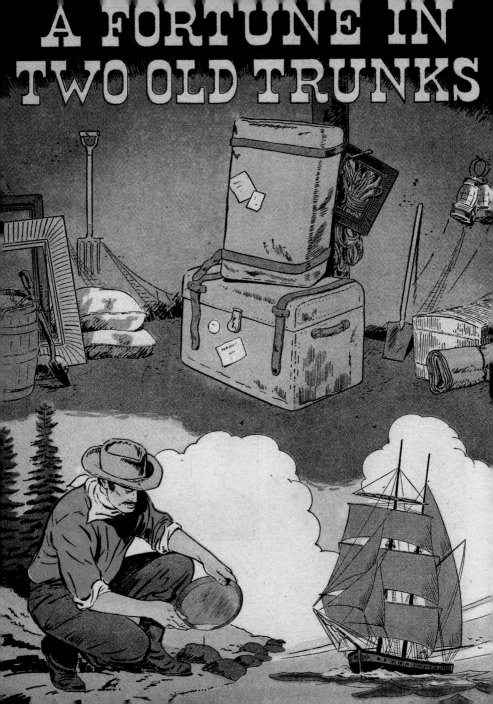

A FORTUNE IN
TWO OLD TRUNKS

"WHAT A SWEET AWAKENING... WHAT A SUBLIME SENSATION...UHM!"

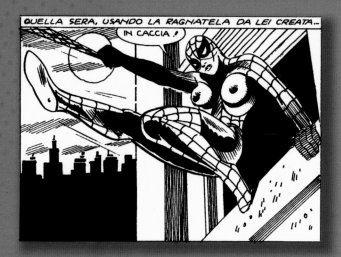

This Italian porno-horror version of *Spider-Man* follows Stan Lee and Steve Ditko's origin but adds some perverse twists. The unsubtly named Virgin Mona is a nerdy virgin at a nuclear research lab. Supervising an experiment overnight, she smashes a jar before a security guard tries to ravish her in her sleep. She is aroused by the radioactive spider she has freed as it starts to penetrate her. In her panic, she crushes the tarantula, whose dying bite down below gives her amazing powers: nymphomania and the unfortunate instinct to strangle her partners whenever she is about to climax. (Luckily she wasn't bitten by the Black Widow species, the female of which eats the male after mating.) Her impractical outfit exposing her breasts and hardly concealing her crotch, she becomes "The Spider Woman," doomed never to reach her first orgasm. Originally published in 1977 by Galassia Editrice, Milan, by issue 10 she had to change to *La Donna Tarantola* (*Tarantula Woman*) and lose the trademark webbing after complaints from Marvel, whose own cleaner Spider-Woman debuted in 1978.

LA DONNA RAGNA NO. 1, 1994, PUBLISHED BY & © EDIZIONI SIRIO, MILAN, ITALY, 100-PAGE B/W DIGEST COMIC. COVER BY PRIMO MARCARINI, WRITER UNCREDITED, INTERIORS DRAWN BY AUGUSTO CHIZZOLI AND MARCELLO TONINELLI

YOU WANT MORE?   SUPERHEROES 110   SEXUALITY 90   RADIATION 122

LA DONNA
RAGNA
FUMETTO PER ADULTI
N.1 - L. 3.000
MORSO

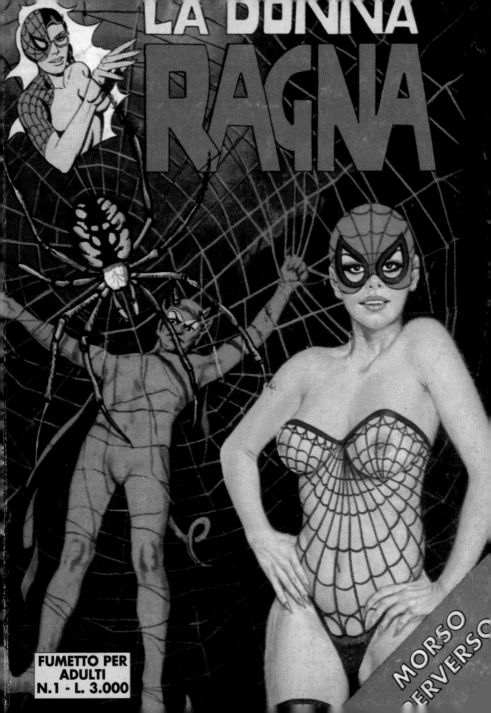

"I'LL BET I COULD SIT HER ON A BARBED WIRE FENCE EVEN -- CAN I TRY SOME AEROBATICS?"

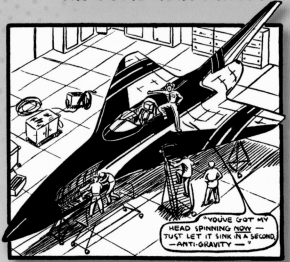

"Those bullets were close!"—and yet Captain Jack keeps his cool throughout this Australian jet-age thriller. No wonder he's been picked out of the whole Air Force to test the top-secret *Spacebird*, the first plane equipped with an anti-gravity machine and auto-control. Jack excels during the test flight until enemy agents fire a missile at *Spacebird*, forcing him to leave the plane on automatic and pursue them on the ground. Captured and locked in the back of a van driven by the agents, Jack is able to use remote control to direct *Spacebird* to drop a hook to pull aside the grille window, setting himself free. Clambering astride the fuselage, he inches back into the cockpit to complete the flight. It ends with smiles all round as Jack's superiors cheerily admit that they set up that near-fatal missile attack themselves "to put you on your mettle." With bosses like that, who needs enemies? One oddity: someone put quotation marks around all the dialogue in the balloons, as if readers wouldn't realize they are reading speech.

TIP-TOP COMICS: WONDER-WINGS SPECIAL NO. 2, 1953, PUBLISHED BY & © SOUTHDOWN PRESS, MELBOURNE, AUSTRALIA, 28-PAGE B/W COMIC. WRITTEN AND DRAWN BY NORMAN CLIFFORD

FEATURE STORY- "CAPTAIN JACK" AND THE "SPACEBIRD."
WONDER-WINGS
COMIC No. 2
d in Australia for trans- by post as a periodical.
"HERE COMES THE SPACEBIRD UNDER THE AUTOMATIC PILOT — AND HERE COME THE ENEMY AGENTS — I'LL BE LUCKY TO GET AWAY, THOSE BULLETS WERE CLOSE!"
ALSO AN EPIC TALE OF ACTION AND ADVENTURE OF WORLD WAR II.
8D

"HE SHORE WUZ A HOPPER AN' A FLOPPER!"

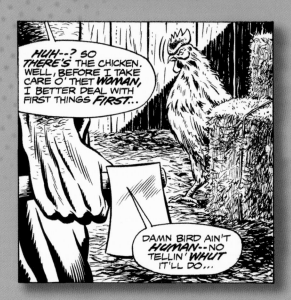

Finally the animals get some vengeance for all their mistreatment from us humans in this bestial variation on EC's *Tales from the Crypt*. In "Let's Play Chicken!" by Doug Moench and Dave Hunt (above), Eben Silica is a cruel Kentucky farmer, who delights in beheading his chickens to see how long their bodies still run around. Eben is also a cruel husband, beating his childless wife and refusing her request to switch from producing poultry to eggs. So Mrs Silica buys some hormones to pump into the hens so that they lay bigger eggs, but Eben stops her, angry that this would spoil the flavour of their flesh. After another battering, Mrs Silica injects one prize hen, which goes on to lay a new breed of strong, intelligent chicken. Once fully grown, it's time for this super-rooster to exact revenge. Tough enough to wield an axe, he decapitates them both and watches how their twitching bodies run around headless, before he sets off to do the same at every farm he comes to. Farmers, beware!

BARN OF FEAR NO. 1, OCTOBER 1977, PUBLISHED BY COMIC ART GALLERY, NEW JERSEY, 44-PAGE B/W COMIC. COVER BY & © ALFREDO P. ALCALA, INTERIORS BY & © VARIOUS WRITERS AND ARTISTS

THE BARN OF FEAR

YOU WANT MORE? CHICKENS 34 ON THE FARM 54 HORROR 106

DO YOU HAVE THE NERVE TO SPEND A RAINY NIGHT
THE BARN OF FEAR
COMIC CAG ART GALLERY
COMIC CAG ART GALLERY
NO. 1
$1.00

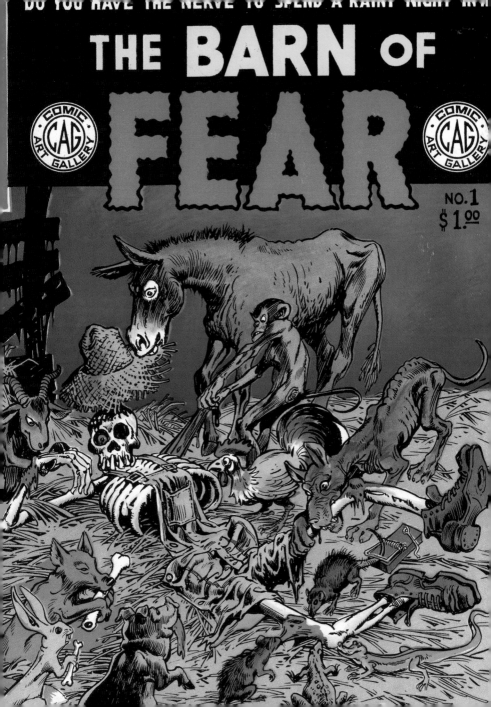

"HIT THE SNOW! IT'S AUNTY FREEZE'S HENCHMEN, THE HOT-LIPPERS!"

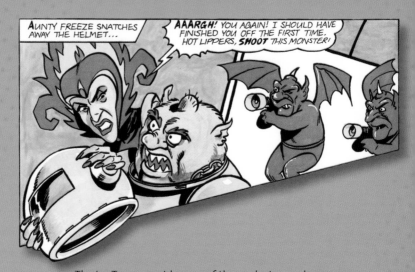

AUNTY FREEZE SNATCHES AWAY THE HELMET...

AAARGH! YOU AGAIN! I SHOULD HAVE FINISHED YOU OFF THE FIRST TIME, HOT LIPPERS, **SHOOT** THIS MONSTER!

The Ice Team must be one of the coolest superhero groups, since they started as lollies or popsicles from Wall's Ice Cream. Their female leader, Sparkle, comes in orange or lemon and Twister is a pineapple spiral laced with lime, while 'Orrible Ogre is blackcurrant. Based on Planet Walls, Sparkle, Twister and surfer buddy Sunsplash zoom to Earth in their spaceship Lol-E-Stix to tackle melting ice-caps and other natural disasters. No, it's not global warming but the heat rays of evil Aunty Freeze. At the North Pole she sets her red-devil Hot-Lippers on the team, but a purple ogre sees them off. He reveals that he is Rex Rocket, rightful ruler of Planet Scorch, usurped by Aunty's spells. Confronting Aunty on her ship, Sparkle's freezing bolts make the witch vanish in clouds of steam. Rex reverts to normal, as do the Hot-Lippers, who turn out to be his two missing brothers. Wall's first superhero, designed for *Eagle* in 1950 by Dan Dare creator Frank Hampson, was Tommy Walls, The Wonder Boy. He got his powers from making a "W" sign with his fingers and eating lots of ice cream.

CHILL NO. 1, 1994, PUBLISHED BY & © WALL'S ICE CREAM, 16-PAGE FREE COMIC. WRITER UNCREDITED, DRAWN BY JOHN RICHARDSON

YOU WANT MORE?   DAIRY 92   FROZEN NORTH 30   SUPERHEROES 12

THE ICE TEAM IN
MELTDOWN ON PLANE
EARTH
FREE
FROM
Wall's
NO.1 '94
Chill

"A VICIOUS EXAMPLE OF THE LENGTHS TO WHICH A DISEASED MIND CAN GO."

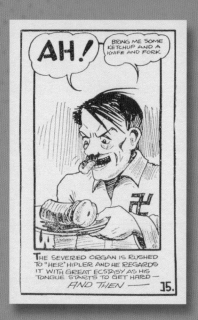

Tijuana Bibles are neither Mexican nor Christian but America's pioneer underground comics: lewd, crude, pocket-sized parodies of fictional and real names in the comics, movies and newspapers, from Popeye or Tarzan to Ingrid Bergman or Gandhi. As many as 1,000 different titles, their print-runs estimated in the millions, were disseminated by clandestine publishers, uncredited cartoonists and illicit distributors from the late Twenties to late Forties. Part satirical smut, part basic sex-education manuals, most take only eight pages to climax. Herr Hitler, however, gets twice that length to be ridiculed as "Her" Hipler, piling onto rumors about his homosexuality the horror of cannibalism. When he catches a Nazi couple having sex in his sanctum, he condemns them to torture and death. The woman offers to be Hitler's slave if he will only spare her lover, but Hitler prefers having his way with boys over breakfast, and she fails to arouse him. The furious Führer orders her lover to be "dis-membered" before her eyes and devours his phallic trophy: "What a connoisseur of edibles he is."

HYME PUTZ PRESENTS "YOU NAZI MAN," UNDATED, LATE 1930S, NO PUBLISHER CREDITED, SMALL 20-PAGE B/W COMIC. WRITTEN AND DRAWN BY "DOC" RANKIN

Hyme Putz
Presents
"YOU NAZI
MAN"

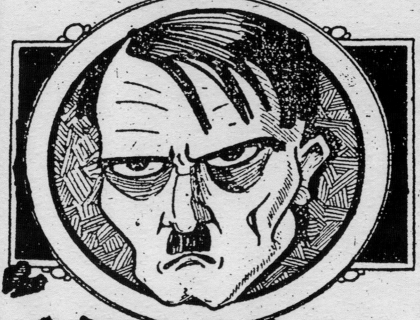

"GO SWIM IN THE LAKE. GO BY NORTH ROAD. CAN'T MISS IT. SWIM IN THE LAKE. VERY REFRESHING. SWIM..."

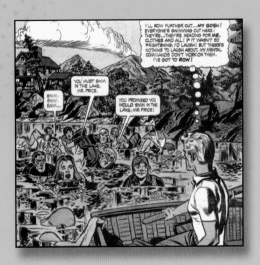

In this creepy Cold War allegory about communism, Matt Price is Brain Boy, the mental marvel of the U.S. secret service. His latest mission is simply to take a vacation. On arrival in the remote Canadian town of Bondooks (population 432), he slowly becomes alarmed by the locals' odd obsession with swimming in their green-tinged lake and their insistence that he does so too. Matt's telepathy reveals that their minds are blank and under mass control. By pretending to join them, he is taken to the spacecraft of the Eerown, which his "great mind" realizes are billions of tiny space monkeys combined into one being, one brain, intent on enslaving the planet. Dropping a radio into a bucket of the green water, Brain Boy stumbles on their weakness: electricity. He wills himself aloft and hurls the radio, on a long extension cord, into the lake, saving humanity.

BRAIN BOY NO. 6, SEPTEMBER–NOVEMBER 1963, PUBLISHED BY & © DELL PUBLISHING CO., NEW YORK, 36-PAGE COMIC. COVER BY VIC PREZIO, WRITTEN BY HERB CASTLE, DRAWN BY FRANK SPRINGER

YOU WANT MORE?   ALIENS 86   COMMIES 94   SPORTS 104

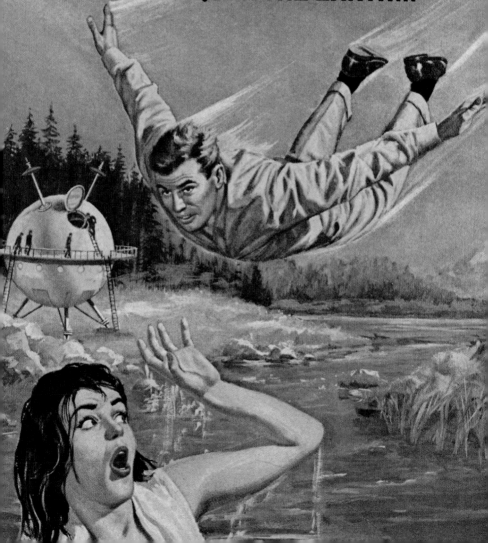

LL®

2c

-075-311

PT.-NOV.

9d

BRAIN BOY

A FANTASTIC SCHEME TO CONQUER THE EARTH...

"TELL ME SON, WHAT'S VERONICA REALLY LIKE?"

WHAT ON AIRTH ARE WE A'WASTIN' TIME FER, PAW... START POKIN'
I THOT I WUZ ...?

Yes, there really was a comic called *SH-T! Comics*. In the grand tradition of pun-filled porn initiated in the late Twenties by the notorious Tijuana Bibles, *SH-T!* lives up to its name and parades the kind of explicit escapades which chaste, sexless family favorites could never get away with in their strips, except perhaps between the panels or in readers' wet dreams. So Milton Caniff's Steve Canyon finally gets it on with his perky cousin Poteet as "Steve Callboy" and "Pusstit" by "Wilton Cantshit." Dale Messick's Brenda Starr uncovers hippy free love as "Brenda Stack by Dale Makesex." Archie by Bob Montana becomes "Starchie by Bob Mountem," who fixes his balding, conservative Dad up so he can have his way with both Betty and Veronica at last. And Fred Lasswell's little hillbilly Snuffy Smith almost gets flattened by Maw's lovemaking in "Sniffy Muff by Fred Asswell." Sniffy seems to speak for most of these repressed characters when he exclaims, "We got lots o' pokin' round t'make up fer lost time." It's all cheerfully puerile and rather quaint by pornographic standards of the era. The fact that the shocking four-letter title itself is censored says a lot.

SH-T! COMICS NO. 1, UNDATED, POSSIBLY EARLY 1970S, NO PUBLISHER DETAILS, PUBLISHED IN AMERICA, 68-PAGE SQUAREBOUND B/W BOOK. WRITER AND ARTIST UNCREDITED

YOU WANT MORE? **PARODY 48** **HILLBILLY 74** **SEXUALITY 56**

No. 1

SH-T!

$3.00

LOOK AT A REAL BARREL O'GOODIES!
Comics for ADULTS ONLY

"THEN ONE OF THE SHADOWS SCUTTLES SILENTLY TOWARD ME LIKE A BLACK SLIMY FOG!"

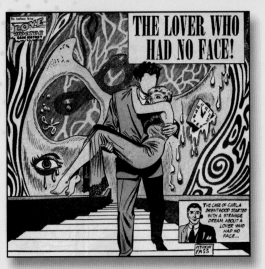

Long before Dr. Ruth, America's post-war boom in marriage guidance led to celebrity counselors like John J. Anthony (former taxi driver Lester Kroll), whose clients could air their troubles in "Mr. Anthony's Love Clinic" radio show and a spin-off comic. Inside most romance comics, bogus experts (usually pseudonyms of the comics' scripters) give advice to the lovelorn in letter columns, so why not give one "love doctor" his own comic? Enter pipe-smoking, silver-templed Dr. Anthony King, treating wealthy Ralph Brentwood and his wife Carla's recurring nightmares: "In the morning, she's always so depressed, she can't look me in the face." Ralph invites Dr. King to meet Carla and she tells him about her dream. In a landscape of dripping clocks and eyeballs, like Salvador Dalí's decor for Hitchcock's *Spellbound*, she is menaced by a shadow until a man with no face rescues her. Our love doctor asks Ralph to lie to Carla that he is going broke. The shock banishes her extreme guilt that she only wanted his money and makes her realize that she married him for love. As Dr. King explains, her faceless savior was Ralph, "as your subconscious wanted him to be—without eyes to see your guilt, without mouth to pronounce judgement." Their marriage saved, the couple leave on their second honeymoon.

DR. ANTHONY KING, HOLLYWOOD LOVE DOCTOR NO. 4, MAY 1954, PUBLISHED BY & © TOBY PRESS, NEW YORK, 36-PAGE COMIC. COVER AND COVER STORY DRAWN BY MYRON FASS, WRITER UNCREDITED

A Sick Heart, A Troubled Mind; "WHO AM I?"
DR. ANTHONY KING,
LOVE DOCTOR
10¢
NO. 4
She lived in a world of fantasy . . . and I couldn't penetrate the mental curtain that made her a stranger to the man she loved.
DR. ANTONY KING

"PREPARE FOR A BLAST, MEN. LET'S HOPE WE GOT FAR ENOUGH AWAY..."

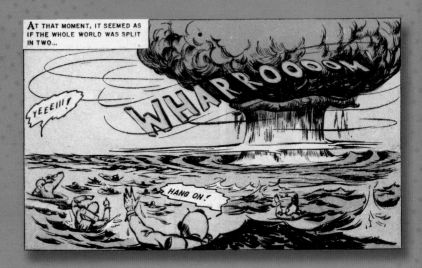

The Korean War was still raging by late 1952, but peace negotiations were progressing, so Youthful Magazines shrewdly upped the ante in their combat comics from *Attack!* to *Atomic Attack!* In came mushroom clouds on the covers, headlines like "I'll Fight in Tomorrow's War," and "True War Stories" about nuclear conflict in the worryingly near future. In "Underwater Inferno" (above) drawn by Vince Napoli, the commies are still threatening the free world in 1976, their moveable base camouflaged as an impregnable iceberg. The United Nations' new atomic submarine, under Commander Packard, is sent to investigate. Thanks to its "anti-sonar coating," the sub shows up as "just a big fish" and gets close enough for Packard to board the iceberg. To his horror, he finds it is fully equipped "as a base for an attack on America!" A U.N. enquiry hails his decision to order the crew to convert the sub's atomic motors into a floating bomb, abandon ship and send it in on autopilot to decimate the Reds' stronghold. Any nasty after-effects from all that radioactive fallout are conveniently ignored.

ATOMIC ATTACK! NO. 7, MAY 1953, PUBLISHED BY & © YOUTHFUL MAGAZINES, NEW YORK, 36-PAGE COMIC. WRITERS AND ARTISTS UNCREDITED

ATOMIC
ATTACK!
UNDERWATER INFERNO
10¢
THE COMMANDOS' LAST RAID!!

"SHE'S GOT THE GASKIN, HOCK AND SHANK OF A GOOD RACER."

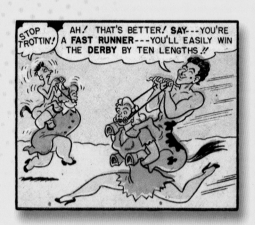

Conceived shortly before baseball legend Babe Ruth's death in 1948, Babe began as an ace baseball-playing variation on hillbilly heartthrob Daisy Mae out of Al Capp's Li'l Abner, but cartoonist Boody Rogers was soon spicing up her tall tales. This cover belies the warped bondage fantasy inside, in which Rogers reverses the roles of Babe astride a centaur and has our hearty heroine being ridden by her four-hooved owner. It all starts when Babe investigates why thousands of the valley's beautiful girls are disappearing on Mystery Mountain. A wolf whistle hypnotizes her into the all-male Centaur Land where she is sold in auction to Pinto Pete, who mounts and rides her, hands tied behind her back, a horse's bit in her mouth. Women are treated like livestock here, kept in stables and fed on hay, worn-out nags doomed to end up in the glue factory. Entering his new prize filly in a steeplechase, Pete agrees to leave Babe's bridle off—"It splits my lips!" She leaps over lethal quicksand, razor blades, red-hot coals and finally off the mountain itself, crashlanding to safety. Oddly, Babe decides to keep her discovery secret, in case people think she's "a ravin' insane idiot," and so leaves all her sisters behind in cruel captivity. The gender politics are off-kilter in another story, where Babe gets plenty of attention from her long-lost female cousin Fanny, in fact film star "Clark Sable" hiding in drag from his admirers. But after Sable endures a smooch by Pappy, a dunking in stale hog lard, a drink of kerosene and other indignities, he flees back to the city, happy to surrender to his rabid fans.

BABE, DARLING OF THE HILLS NO. 8, OCTOBER 1949, PUBLISHED BY FEATURE PUBLICATIONS, NEW YORK, 52-PAGE COMIC. WRITTEN AND DRAWN BY & © GORDON "BOODY" ROGERS
NOTE: THE "MYSTERY MOUNTAIN" STORY WAS REPRINTED IN RAW VOL. 2, NO. 2 (PENGUIN, 1990)

YOU WANT MORE?   BONDAGE 36   MYTHIC BEINGS 88   HILLBILLY 68

BABE, DARLING OF THE HILLS
Oct.
No.8
10c
52 PAGES
WHERE TO, BABE ?
OH, JEST ENY PLACE---IT'S SO RO-MAN-TICK T' GO DRIVIN' WIF YUH IN TH' MOONLIGHT !!

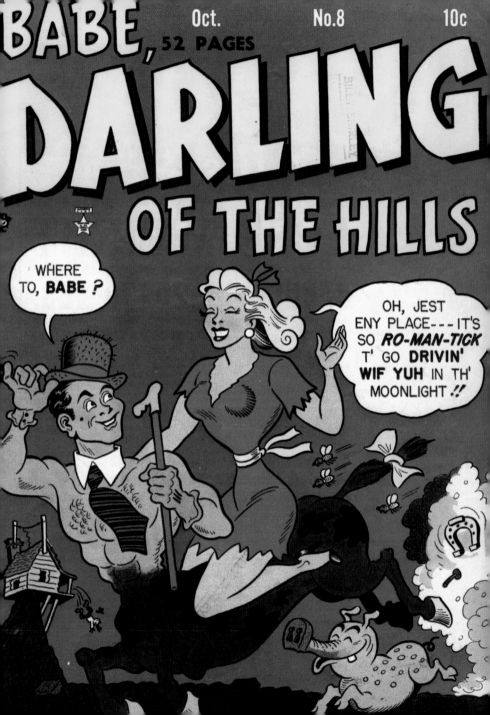

"ALL THIS FROM ONE LI'L PACK O' BUTTS."

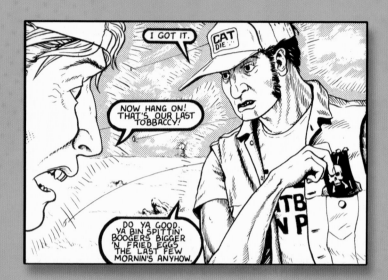

While most tobacco industry giants tried to deny the dangers and pass off their brands as cool lifestyle accessories, The Enlightened Tobacco Company were chillingly honest in 1991 about the lethal effects of smoking. Their Death™ cigarettes came in funereal black packets bearing a skull-and-crossbones, which both emphasized their perils and cunningly celebrated their badness. As part of their merchandising, which included a coffin-shaped gift box, they produced this comic. At the White Plains airbase in Arizona, abandoned after an alien attack, dumb "bruthas" Dwight and Todd accidentally set off "some kinda Com'nist space-time travelin' gizmo" which zaps them back to the Middle Ages. Here, the last pack of Death™ cigarettes they leave behind distorts history, as it becomes a holy relic for a smoking religion. Grabbing back their smokes, they return to find the present altered too and the airbase one gigantic Death™ cigarettes factory. That fantasy success never came to be, though, as the company folded in 1999.

ME & MAH BRUTHA IN WHITE PLAINS, DARK AGES, UNDATED (MID-1990S), PUBLISHED BY & © THE ENLIGHTENED TOBACCO COMPANY PLC, LONDON, 16-PAGE FREE B/W COMIC MAGAZINE. WRITTEN BY MIKE JAY, DIALOGUE BY B.J. CUNNINGHAM AND DRAWN BY RICHARD CAMPLING

YOU WANT MORE?   ON THE ROAD 90   UP IN SMOKE 18   DESERT 48

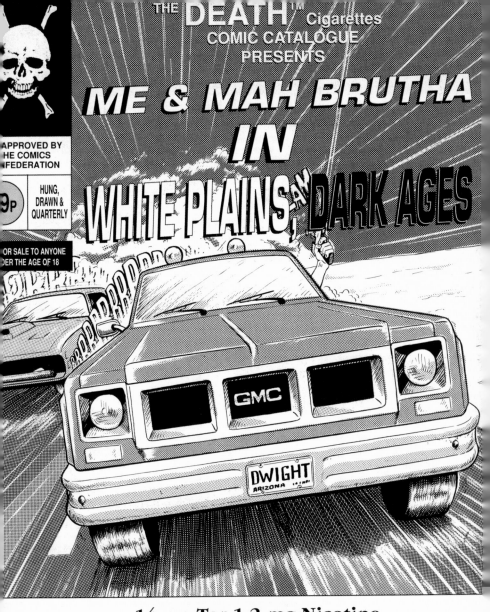

14 mg Tar 1.2 mg Nicotine

Health Departments' Chief Medical Officers: **SMOKING KILLS.**

SMOKING CAUSES CANCER, HEART DISEASE AND OTHER FATAL
DISEASES. SMOKING WHEN PREGNANT HARMS YOUR BABY.
PROTECT CHILDREN: DON'T MAKE THEM BREATHE YOUR SMOKE.

"AND HOW ABOUT A GORILLA TO TACKLE THOSE VIET CONG GUERILLAS?"

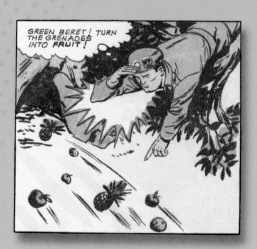

Harking back to young Billy Batson transforming into the adult Captain Marvel by saying "Shazam!", writer Otto Binder came up with this gung-ho Sixties variation. Eager Tod Holton is given his Uncle Roger's former beret to which a jungle wizard has pinned a magic amulet. Whenever Tod puts it on, he changes into Super Green Beret "to battle on the side of good against evil oppressors in all warfare" and can channel the wizard's magical powers simply by saluting. Touching the beret, Tod picks up "telepathy messages" alerting him to trouble. His first mission whisks him off to Viet Nam where he saves some besieged, starving American troops by turning the enemy's grenades into oranges and pineapples. Further assignments take him to Latin America to help rebels depose a dictator modeled on Fidel Castro, and back in time to prevent Hitler escaping, the day before he is due to die. Despite the limitless possibilities of using magic, Tod, a teen in an adult's body, regularly prefers brute force. With public opinion turning against the war, Tod hung up his beret after two issues.

SUPER GREEN BERET NO. 1, APRIL 1967, PUBLISHED BY & © MILSON PUBLISHING COL, INC., ST. LOUIS, MISSOURI, 68-PAGE COMIC. WRITTEN BY OTTO BINDER, DRAWN BY CARL PFEUFER

No. 1
APR. 1967
25¢
TOD HOLTON
SUPER
GREEN
BERET
APPROVED BY THE COMICS CODE AUTHORITY
GIANT SIZED
ACTION
IKE
O ACTION
VER
BEFORE!
THE CURTAIN RISES ON A NEW WAR HERO! NOT A TOUGH VETERAN ENLISTEE! NO, IT IS A TEEN-AGE BOY, TOO YOUNG TO ENLIST, WHO CREATES AMAZING LEGENDS AS A SUPER-SOLDIER BY MEANS OF FANTASTIC SUPER POWERS!
CRACK!
STORIES

"OLIVE ALWAYS SPENDS HOURS IN THE BEAUTY PARLOR! IT DOESN'T DO MUCH GOOD! ARF! ARF!"

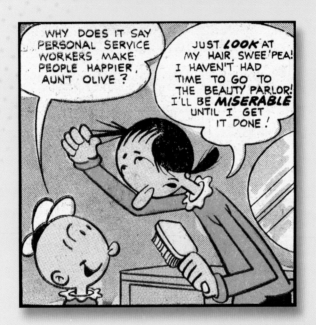

It would be hard to come up with a less appropriate cartoon star to be a spokesperson for career opportunities in personal services that the brawny, uncouth, pop-eyed sailor-man Popeye, and yet here he is extolling the career opportunities for barbers, beauticians, manicurists and masseurs. Along the way, we get a flashback to Popeye as a boy with long, rather girlish blond locks and, of course, his perpetual pipe, as he gets a terrible pudding-basin haircut. He goes on to explain how to become a chauffeur, marriage counselor, psychologist, child care attendant, school bus driver, social worker and vet. And for a final flourish, the back cover reveals Popeye with Olive Oyl enjoying the new health salon opened by, of all people, his big, bearded arch-enemy, Brutus.

POPEYE AND PERSONAL SERVICE CAREERS, 1972, PUBLISHED BY & © KING FEATURES, NEW YORK, 36-PAGE COMIC. COVER BY GEORGE WILDMAN, WRITTEN BY JOE GILL, DRAWN BY FRANK ROBERGE

YOU WANT MORE?   CAREERS 26   INJURIES 42   GORGEOUSNESS 46

KING

POPEYE and PERSONAL SERVICE CAREERS

THERE IS NOTHING LIKE A HAIRCUT, SHAVE AND MANICURE TO MAKE ME FEEL GOOD!
I HAVE A HEAVY DATE WITH OLIVE OYL TONIGHT! ARF! ARF!
Albert

"YOU CAN DO SOME GREAT THINGS THAT REGULAR WOMEN CAN'T DO, 'CAUSE THEY'RE LACKING ONE OF THESE ACTIVE THIGH STUBS."

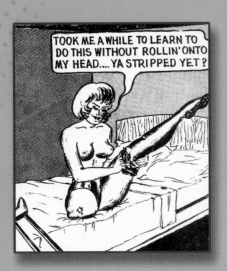

Sassy secretary Lyn thinks her sex life is over when she loses her right leg in a car crash and is dumped by her boyfriend, but with tutelage from Sheri, an amputee volunteer aide at rehab, she comes to cherish her uniquely desirable state as a "foxy amp chick." Moving in together, Sheri wises Lyn up to all sorts of solutions, such as painting different "sticks" ("You never call 'em crutches") to match her outfits, or using the Shoe Swap Club to get more left shoes. It's not long before Lyn finds a guy who appreciates "stump play" and with her settlement money she buys a fancy customized automobile. Her experiences climax in a poolside orgy with no sticks, limbs or other fittings allowed. Rene, the authoress of this empowering erotic manual, is a double amputee and her husband Rich draws the illustrations.

AMPUTEE LOVE NO. 1, 1975, PUBLISHED BY & © LAST GASP, BERKELEY, CALIFORNIA, 36-PAGE B/W COMIC. COVER BY BRENT BOATES, INTERIORS WRITTEN BY RENE AND DRAWN BY RICH

YOU WANT MORE?   SEXUALITY 68   ORGIES 20   INJURIES 112

AMPUTEE
LOVE
ADULTS
$2.00
ONLY
LAST GASP

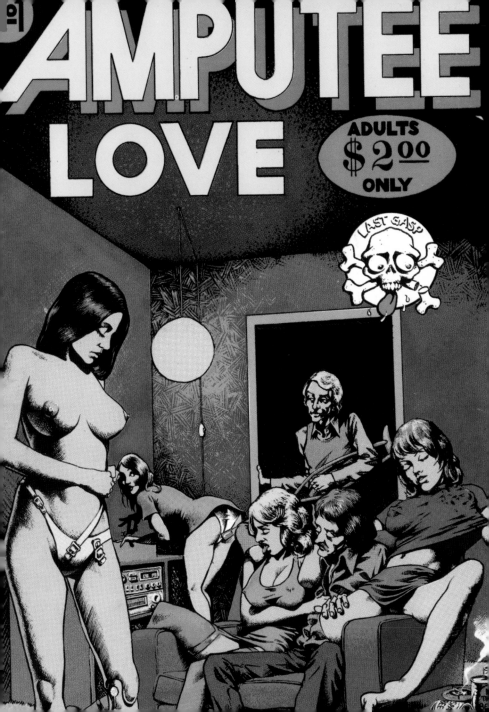

KOOKIE

"A RING FIT FOR A PRINCESS! A MAGNIFICENT JADE MEATBALL ON AN EXQUISITELY WROUGHT NEST OF CERAMIC SPAGHETTI! LET ME SLIP IT ON YOUR FINGER..."

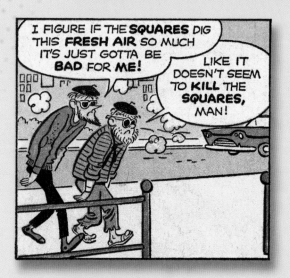

This is what happens when mainstream America co-opts the beat movement. Berets, bongos and beards fill this beatnik comedy from the normally wholesome and "square" Dell Comics. The pretty, naïve blonde Kookie works as a waitress at Mama Pappa's Expresso coffee house. Her bohemian customers include jeweler Jason with his spaghetti-and-meatball ring, poet Fleahaven who serenades *Annie P. McGooey*, a tugboat, and sculptor Herman who pours Mama's coffee on his stone to make it easier to carve. Supporting players include double-act Bongo and Bop and Mama's 86-year-old lecherous landlord Mr Flipside. Beatsploitation from the pen of John Stanley, best known for Little Lulu.

KOOKIE NO. 1, FEBRUARY—APRIL 1962, PUBLISHED BY & © DELL PUBLISHING CO., INC., NEW YORK, 36-PAGE COMIC. WRITTEN AND LAID OUT BY JOHN STANLEY, DRAWN BY BILL WILLIAMS

YOU WANT MORE?   HIPPIES 52   POP MUSIC 24   FOOD 54

DELL
15¢
B.—APR.
KOOKIE
M-A-A-N!!

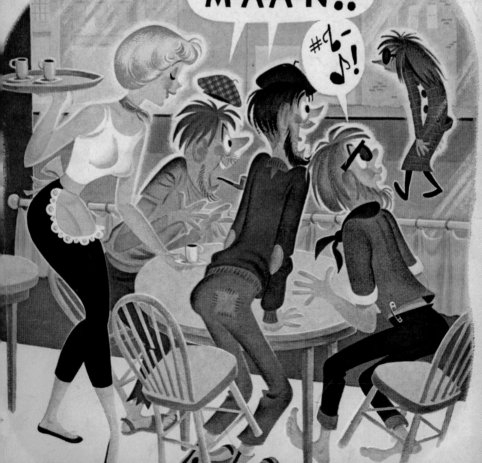

"SORRY BOYS, BUT THE SCALES ARE WEIGHTED IN MY FAVOR!"

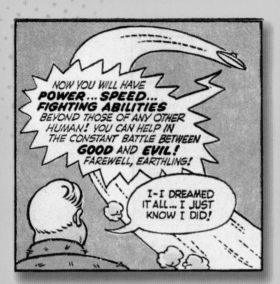

No makeovers or extreme diets, thank you—this superhero likes being super-sized. Voracious zillionaire hobbyist Van Crawford spots an out-of-control flying saucer and topples a tree for it to land in safely. The saucer morphs into a green alien who explains that this was no accident but a test of empathy, wits and speed. In reward, he hands Crawford a chocolate drink which grants him special powers, including transforming into a flying saucer. When spies try to steal him, Van reverts to human form and captures them. Their insult, "Fatman," inspires his new identity and new hobby—being a costumed crimefighter. His first foe is the tragic Anti-Man, a "Black Lagoon"-type creature angry at humans for making him "the last of my race." Fatman finds an ally in stringbean Lucius Pindle, alias metal-coated Tinman, but their battle is called off when the far bigger Mrs. Anti-Man arrives to scold her "miserable tadpole" of a husband. "Every time he gets hopped-up on seaweed juice, he tells that tale!" She carries him off home because he has to find supper for "our 5,000 children."

FATMAN THE HUMAN FLYING SAUCER NO. 1, APRIL 1967, PUBLISHED BY & © LIGHTNING COMICS/MILSON PUBLISHING CO., INC., NEW YORK, 68-PAGE COMIC. WRITTEN BY OTTO BINDER, DRAWN BY C.C. BECK

YOU WANT MORE?   FATTIES 90   ALIENS 40   SUPERHEROES 62

ROVED THE MICS ODE THORITY
PR.1967
25¢
No. 1
FATMAN THE HUMAN FLYING SAUCER
TIME TO CHANGE TO...
FATMAN THE HUMAN
THE ONLY COMIC HERO WITH 3 IDENTITIES
FLYING SAUCER!
Featuring ANTI-MAN
MONSTROUS SEA HORROR
Introducing TINMAN teen-age hero
WRITTEN & DRAWN BY THE CREATORS OF THE ORIGINAL CAPTAIN MARVE

"FRIEND, BLOW THE FIRE IN THE OTHER DIRECTION, I WISH TO SLEEP PEACEFULLY."

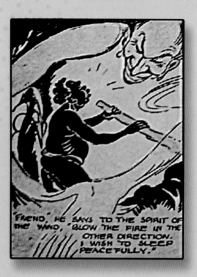

"In Australia's Far Northern Wilderness dwell the remnants of the tribes which held the land before the coming of the whites." Growing up there on their family's vast, remote cattle stations, the Durack sisters love the outback and the dreamtime tales they hear from its Aborigine inhabitants. In 1942, Mary and Elizabeth were the first to incorporate Aboriginal art techniques, colors and motifs to re-create these stories as comics for the *Sunday Telegraph* in Sydney. Our guides are Nungalla and his longer-haired sister Jungalla, children of the Mirriwun tribe. In "The Young White Chief" (above), they protect a lost son of white settlers who has seized weapons sticking out from the grave of the tribe's recently buried chieftain and been hailed as his reincarnation. Gunyi, the usurped new chief, starts a bush fire to kill the boy, but he is saved by the Spirit of Wind, summoned by the children's ally Murrabingi with his bamboo trumpet. The son's safe return brings the tribe and settlers together in celebration.

A BOOK OF PICTURE STORIES, CIRCA 1943, PUBLISHER UNCREDITED, 60-PAGE BOARD-COVERED COMIC. WRITTEN BY & © MARY DURACK, DRAWN BY & © ELIZABETH DURACK

YOU WANT MORE? **MYTHIC BEINGS 96 AUSTRALIA 58 DREAMS 70**

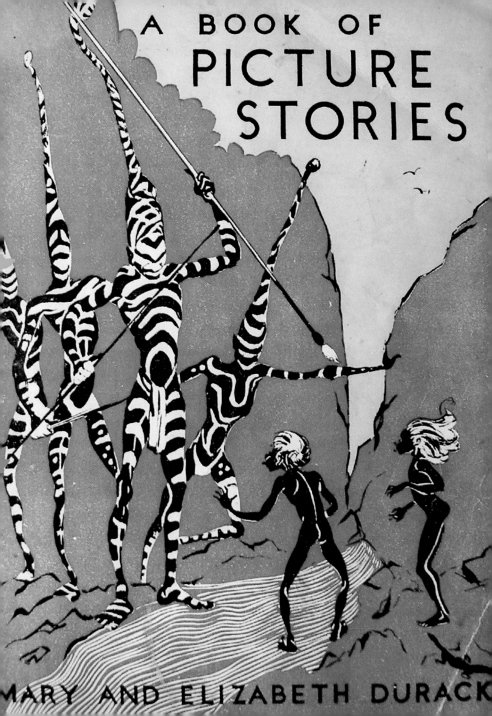

A BOOK OF PICTURE STORIES

MARY AND ELIZABETH DURACK

"YOU GAVE US A ROOM WITH ONLY ONE BED! ARE YOU TRYING TO CALL US FAGS OR SOMETHING?"

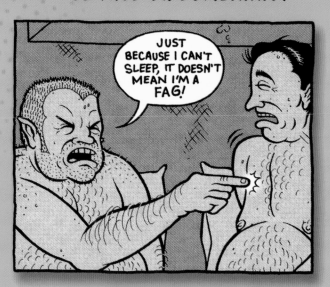

In this poignant fable of "muddled ethics, misguided aggression and searing hypocrisy," bachelors Butch and Petey have been long-haul trucking together for more than a decade. Well past their prime and severely sexually frustrated, they hold little appeal to women—"Who needs 'em, anyway?"—and hate all kinds of people, but especially fags. One night, they have no choice but to share a bed in a motel. Unable to sleep, Butch is alarmed to find that the smell of Petey's socks gives him his first erection in almost ten years. Cupids fill the room as a night of passion ensues. The morning after, seeing penises wherever they look, they vent their confusion by brawling and get thrown in jail, where they justify further intimacies as "robust, manly enjoyment." On release, the homosexual homophobes get away with a gay murder rampage and yet somehow they continue to act like fags and deny it.

TRUCKER FAGS IN DENIAL, JUNE 2004, PUBLISHED BY FANTAGRAPHICS BOOKS, INC, SEATTLE, 36-PAGE B/W COMIC. WRITTEN BY & © JIM GOAD, DRAWN BY & © JIM BLANCHARD

YOU WANT MORE?   GAY 64   ON THE ROAD 26   FATTIES 116

TRUCKER FAGS
IN DENIAL
RT BY
IM BLANCHARD
STORY BY
JIM GOAD
ADULTS ONLY
$3.95 USA
$6.00 CAN.
FANTAGRAPHICS BOOKS
I-C BUTZ

"I'M TALKING ABOUT THAT JUNKY BACON YOU'VE BEEN USING! HOW DO YOU EXPECT US TO EAT THAT STUFF?"

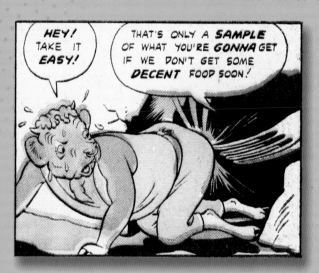

Elsie the Cow was dreamt up in the 1930s as the Borden Company's mascot to promote their dairy products. She bears a striking resemblance to French cheese character The Laughing Cow, created in 1921. Elsie became a celebrity across North America, appearing at the 1939 and 1964—65 New York World's Fairs and in the 1940 RKO movie *Little Men*. The heffer housewife's ring-nosed hubby was Elmer Bull, who was corralled into endorsing Borden's milk-protein-based adhesive, Elmer's Glue-All. While they mostly get involved in light domestic comedy with their daughter Beulah and son Beauregard, in one loopy tale a chemistry set shrinks Elmer down to the size of a mouse. The mice are upset over the "junky bacon" he's leaving in the mousetraps and stab him in the butt with a fork. Restored to normal, he buys new traps, bacon and a pound of (presumably Borden) cheese, the only mention of the benefits of milk produce in this comic.

ELSIE THE COW NO.1, NOVEMBER 1949, PUBLISHED BY BELL FEATURES LTD, TORONTO, ONTARIO, 36-PAGE COMIC. "ELSIE" IS © & ™ BDS TWO, INC. & BORDEN, INC. WRITER AND ARTIST UNCREDITED

YOU WANT MORE?   DAIRY 116   CRITICS 96   DEAR DADS 118

NEW! NEW! LAUGH WITH AMERICA'S No. 1 FAMILY
CAN. ED.
10c
Elsie
the cow
Vol. 1, No. 1
COMICS
a BIG
EXTRA VALUE
magazine!
Home
THE BULLETIN

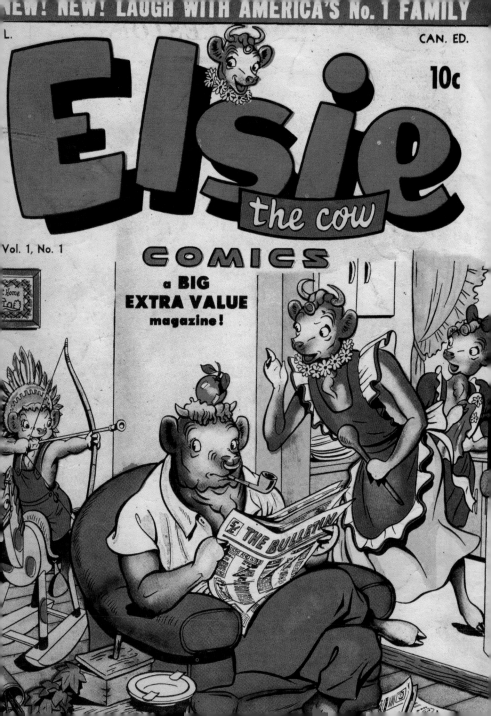

"GAULLEFINGER IS JUST ANOTHER SUPER-VILLAIN WITH A BIG NOSE."

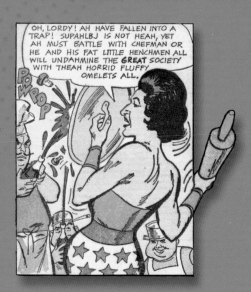

World leaders had been transformed into superheroes before. British Prime Minister Harold Macmillan came to be identified with Supermac, a caricature by Vicky (Victor Weisz) in 1958, and an animated Super President, the fictional James Norcross, played for one season in 1967 on American Saturday-morning TV. But here's an entire pun-filled satirical comic about costumed versions of U.S. President Lyndon B. Johnson, alias SuperLBJ, and his cabinet, who team up as G.R.E.A.T. ("Group Resigned to End All Threats") against an array of supervillains, from France's Gaullefinger (DeGaulle) to Russia's Dr. Nyet (Khrushchev). Leaping into action because "SuperLBJ Is Missing!" the team including LBJ's wife, "Lady Bird" Johnson, as Wonderbird (above), Barry Goldwater as Colonel America and Hubert Humphrey as Captain Marvelous, fail to find him, so it's up to SuperLBJ to save himself and then the entire world. Plotting behind the scenes are Bobman and Teddy, or Robert and Ted Kennedy, who starred in a sequel of their own.

THE GREAT SOCIETY COMIC BOOK, 1966, PUBLISHED BY PARALLAX COMIC BOOKS, INC., NEW YORK, 36-PAGE COMIC. WRITTEN BY & © D.J. ARNESON, DRAWN BY & © TONY TALLARICO

ARALLAX
BOOK COMPANY
AND POCKET BOOKS INC.
#10135
THE GREAT SOCIETY
COMIC BOOK
D.J. ARNESON
AND
NY TALLARICO
WHY....THAT, THAT COULD BE A GREAT SOCIETY!
SUPER LBJ
LBJ

"THIS IS PROBABLY UNCOMFORTABLE. SHOULD I TAKE IT OFF?"

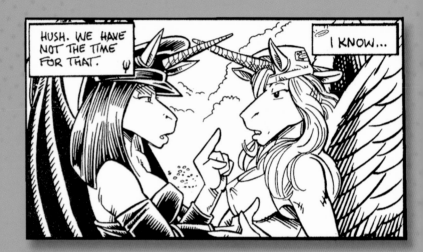

"Furries" are people with varying degrees of interest in anthropomorphic animals, real or imaginary. For some furries that interest can include sexual attraction, which may be expressed through erotic fantasy comics, sometimes of a highly specialized appeal. In Dashe's cover story, a unicorn pupil at St. Wilhelmina's School for Girls walks into a basement classroom expecting to be interviewed for the Drama Club, but winds up being initiated by a stern unicorn mistress and her pupils into a lesbian clique. Their error comes to light when the real recruit knocks on the door, a rather butch rhino girl in glasses and pigtails. In another romp by Max Lowell Voltage (above), a bat-winged leather unicorn from hell steals a moment of passion with her forbidden opposite, an angel-winged blonde unicorn from heaven. By the way, the "extra large" refers to the size of the issue, not the lesbian unicorns.

GENUS NO. 20: SPECIAL EXTRA LARGE LESBIAN UNICORN ISSUE, SEPTEMBER 1996, PUBLISHED BY VENUS COMICS/ANTARCTIC PRESS, SAN ANTONIO, TEXAS, 52-PAGE B/W COMIC. COVER BY & © DASHE, PANEL BY & © MAX LOWELL VOLTAGE, OTHER INTERIORS BY VARIOUS

YOU WANT MORE?   MYTHIC BEINGS 74   CRITTERS 96   LESBIANS 36

ADULT READERS
VENUS COMICS™
No. 20
SEPT. 1996
$3.95 U.S.
$5.50 Canadian
GENUS™
SPECIAL EXTRA LARGE LESBIAN UNICORN ISSUE

"SHE LOOKS LIKE THOSE PIN-UP GIRLS THE EARTH MEN GO FOR!"

COSMO THE MERRY MARTIAN

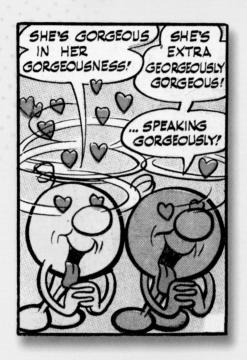

Launched from wholesome Archie Comics in 1958, not long before the Soviets' Sputnik satellite accelerated in the space race, was the rather phallic-looking Cosmo the Merry Martian. His fourth instalment begins with Cosmo and his assorted alien companions on foggy Venus being carried by hairy orange giants to the volcano palace of the planet's ruler. Cosmo upsets his jealous Martian girlfriend Astra when he goes google-eyed at the Queen of Venus in her strapless swimsuit and high-heel boots. Lovely but lonely, she picks Cosmo to be her King and eternal prisoner, but Cosmo really loves Astra. It's up to bearded Professor Thimk to devise a rescue plan, with help from cowardly Orbi, the squabbling moonlings, yellow and orange and both called Oog, the flying Gillywump, Astra and space-pup Jojo. Distracting the giant guards and using rocket packs, they whisk Cosmo to their spaceship, but take off in such a hurry that the controls jam and send them next straight to Saturn. This quirky sci-fi serial ended on another cliffhanger with the sixth issue.

COSMO THE MERRY MARTIAN NO. 4, JUNE 1959, PUBLISHED BY & © ARCHIE COMICS, NEW YORK, 36-PAGE COMIC. WRITTEN AND DRAWN BY BOB WHITE

YOU WANT MORE?   ROMANCE 6   ALIENS 66   GORGEOUSNESS 124

RCHIE
ERIES
COSMO
APPROV
BY THE
COMIC
CODE
AUTHORI
JUNE
10¢
THE MERRY MARTIAN
PDC
VENUS
ONE OF YOU SHALL BE MY KING!
DON'T YOU DARE EVEN LOOK AT VENUS, COSMO, OR I'LL CROWN YOU!

"SOME SORTA MUTILATED DOG CARCASS! HEAD WAS STUCK ON A STAKE! ALL BURNED! WEIRD SATANIC THING, I GUESS..."

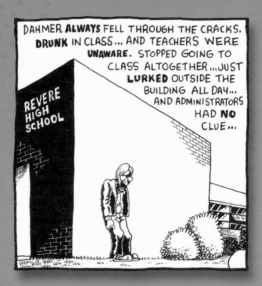

"You went to school with Dahmer, the serial killer? What was he like?" Cartoonist Derf's memoir offers no gory exploitation, just the far more chilling ordinariness of misfit teenagers enduring "the hormonal hell that is Junior High" in 1978. The 15-year-old Dahmer comes across as painfully shy, bullied and dysfunctional, numbing himself with beer, collecting roadkill to dissect and dissolve in acid. He becomes invisible to all except Derf and a few nerdy classmates, and they treat Dahmer warily, not as their buddy but as a weirdo mascot who shows off as a "spastic freak." With all those warning signs, Derf asks how everyone could have been so blind: "Imagine, no friends, no real connection to others, incapable of even having a normal conversation, totally utterly alone. Would that drive YOU mad?"

MY FRIEND DAHMER, MARCH 2002, PUBLISHED BY DERFCITY COMICS, CLEVELAND, OHIO, 28-PAGE B/W COMIC. WRITTEN AND DRAWN BY & © DERF, ALIAS JOHN BACKDERF

YOU WANT MORE?   MADNESS 32   PROBLEM KIDS 30   OUTSIDERS 116

DERFCITY COMICS

$2.95 USA
$4.50 CAN.

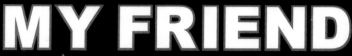

MY FRIEND

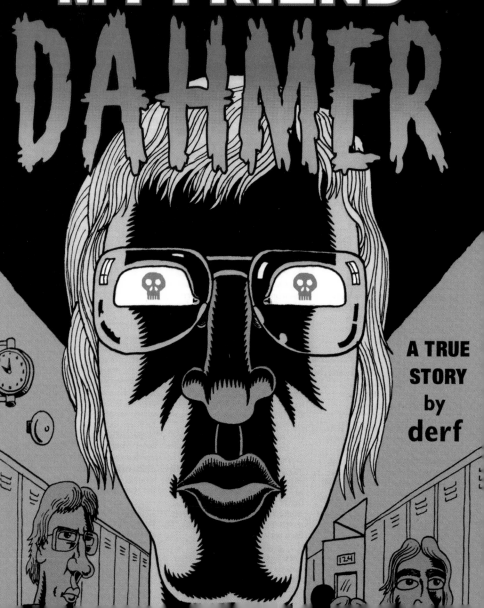

DAHMER

A TRUE
STORY
by
derf

JUST MARRIED

"DAD WOULD HAVE A FIT IF HE KNEW A JEWISH BOY WAS TRYING TO KISS ME, DAVID!"

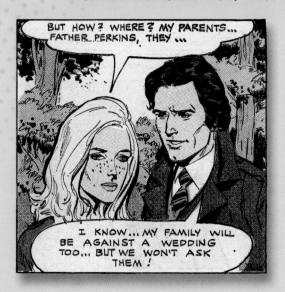

The formula for American romance comics, especially once the Comics Code Authority scrubbed them clean from 1955, was mainly one-off stories with lots of tears, no controversy, and usually a happy ending and a clinch by the last panel. Changes came slowly, but by the late Sixties they tried tackling some topical issues, like race, women's lib, and in this unusual serialized saga the mixed-faith marriage of Jewish boy David Goldman to Irish Catholic Eileen O'Brien. In "Heartache Ahead" the two lovers decide to elope and marry, but when they phone home from the honeymoon suite, their parents, especially David's Orthodox dad and Eileen's "rednecked" father, are furious and storm into their hotel room at 1.30am for a mighty row. The episode ends with the newlyweds kissing, oblivious to the furore, as their two mothers confer. Next issue? "Fresh problems, and even greater joy, as they begin their married life together!"

JUST MARRIED NO. 93, MARCH 1973, PUBLISHED BY & © CHARLTON PRESS INC., DERBY, CONNECTICUT, 36-PAGE COMIC. WRITTEN BY JOE GILL, DRAWN BY A. MARTINEZ AND J. ZUÑIGA

YOU WANT MORE?   CHRISTIANITY 112   ROMANCE 70   DEAR DADS 108

ALL NEW
JUST
FREE POSTER!
BRIAN FORSTER
SEE INSIDE
APPROVED BY THE COMICS CODE AUTHORITY
RLTON
OMICS
0274-373
NO. 93
MAR.
CDC
ONLY
20¢
MARRIED
T&P 6p
SHOULD A JEWISH BOY AND AN IRISH GIRL FALL IN LOVE? BEGINNING IN THIS ISSUE THE CONTINUING STORY OF DAVID and EILEEN...
"Heart-Ache Ahead"

"GIVE ME YOUR BEST GAME. AND IF YOU BREATHE ON ME. I'M GONNA TAKE IT PERSONAL."

GODZILLA VS. BARKLEY

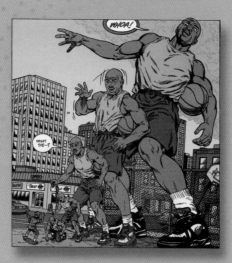

Of all the gigantic opponents which the Japanese movie-monster Godzilla has faced, surely the most bizarre must be American basketball star Charles Barkley. They first met in a brief but mythic 30-second commercial for Nike's Air Ballistic Force line of basketball shoes, which premiered September 9, 1992 on MTV. The bigger story was only revealed a year later in this comic. So how does Barkley grow so tall? The fervent belief of Matthew, his biggest fan, that the player is "Earth's greatest warrior," combined with the gift of his grandpa's magic silver dollar, make Barkley rocket up to skyscraper height. Calling Godzilla a "sorry, suitcase-lookin' sucker," Barkley goads him away from threatening the city to play a game at the old space-shuttle airfield, using the gantry for a hoop. Understandably, Godzilla gets grouchy at Barkley trouncing him and melts the ball with his atomic breath. Yet they wind up buddies after he gets the monster a huge pair of 13,000 EEE sneakers and leaves him doing a million lay-ups.

GODZILLA VS. BARKLEY, DECEMBER 1993, PUBLISHED BY DARK HORSE COMICS, MILWAUKIE, OREGON, 36-PAGE COMIC, © DARK HORSE, CHARLES BARKLEY ENTERPRISES, INC., TOHO CO., LTD. GODZILLA ® & © TOHO CO., LTD. COVER BY DAVE DORMAN, WRITTEN BY MIKE BARON, ART BY JEFF BUTLER & KEITH AIKEN

YOU WANT MORE?   DINOSAURS 122   SPORTS 38   GIANTS 110

DARK HORSE COMICS
GODZILLA VS. BARKLEY
$2.95 US
$3.70 CAN
GODZILLA
VS.
BARKLEY
READ IN AWE AS
GODZILLA
BATTLES
CHARLES BARKLEY
IN A CATACLYSMIC
GAME OF HOOPS THE

"YOUR TYPE GIVE US REAL BIKERS A BAD NAME!!"

THE ADVENTURES OF FTW

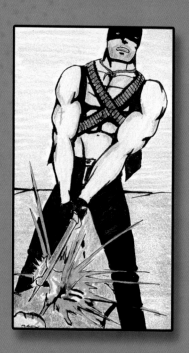

In a tribal near-future London, meat-eating hard men FTW (or "F*** The World") and Hatchet can't enjoy their T-bone steaks without being pestered with "Meat is Murder" leaflets from Brixton's smelly vegetarian hippies. Forcing one of them to eat his own castrated member, the leather-clad bikers spark off an all-out street war. They upgrade their motorcycles with "some new toys," which they exchange for cocaine from an addicted Arthur Daley (George Cole from TV's *Minder*), and then roar off to wreak havoc on all and sundry, assisted by their Rottweiler Hardly. It all ends with Hatchet captured and FTW vowing, "I'll be back!" but issue 2, with "the chance to win a superb Honda 650 Chop," never appeared. What the crayon-colored art inside may lack in polish is more than made up for by its slasher-film gore and sheer testosterone-fuelled compulsion.

THE ADVENTURES OF FTW NO. 1, 1993, PUBLISHED BY & © BAD ASS PUBLICATIONS LTD., ST. LEONARDS-ON-SEA, ENGLAND, 36-PAGE COMIC MAGAZINE. CREATED BY NEIL GALLAHER, COVER BY MARC DANDO, INTERIOR DRAWN BY LEWIS PARKS

YOU WANT MORE?   HORROR 28   BIKERS 52   LONDON 38

THE ADVENTURES OF
FTW
BAD ASS
PULICATIONS
LTD.
£2.00
Volume 1 Issue 1
Not to be sold to minors
or smelly bloody hippies.

"COULD IT BE -- SOMEONE TRYING TO STEAL OUR J-JAR?"

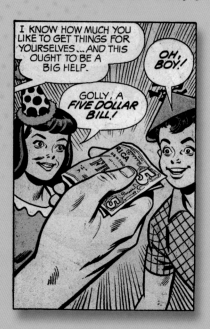

Johnny and Judy are good junior savers, making money by baby-sitting, delivering newspapers, washing Dad's car, and stashing their cash in a big glass jar for the day they can afford new bikes. But it's not the most practical container. When the jar breaks, they lose some coins down a heating vent. After they read news of a big robbery, "they also found out what it meant to worry," becoming so paranoid that they take their jar with them on vacation. Homeward bound, their parents drop them off at an amusement park where the temptations of hotdogs, pop, ice cream and the rides wipe out their nest egg. "Conscience-stricken and miserable," the kids break down and confess. Rather than scold them, Dad takes them down to the local Savings and Loan Association. Leering Mr Strong is only too pleased to look after their money, which will be secure in a vault and earn them interest—"like getting an extra allowance!" In no time "the money just seems to pile up like magic" to buy those bikes and they become hooked on "the saving habit!"

$AVING CAN BE FUN!, 1968, PUBLISHED BY & © THE SAVINGS AND LOAN FOUNDATION, INC., WASHINGTON, D.C., 20-PAGE FREE COMIC. WRITER UNCREDITED, DRAWN BY CHIC STONE

YOU WANT MORE?   DEAR DADS 26   GOOD ADVICE 14   CHILDREN 42

$AVING CAN BE FUN!

COMMENDED by PARENTS' MAGAZINE AS ADVERTISED THEREIN

58-0874
SAVINGS & LOAN ASSOCIATION
SAFETY OF YOUR SAVINGS

"THIS WALRUS... MUST BE FIFTY METERS LONG!"

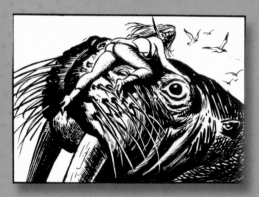

Cold War secrecy meant that there was little reliable information about state-controlled life behind the Iron Curtain in the 1960s. Dissident Czech author Petr Sadecky knew that publishing in Britain sensational smuggled evidence of a "Progressive Political Pornography" group in Kiev, who had somehow dared to print wild samizdat underground comics critical of the Soviet regime, would fire Westerners' romantic notions of young intellectual rebels in Russia. Especially as their heroine Octobriana was "a kind of Russian Barbarella," with her Mongol features, unibrow and hairy armpits, blonde topknot, snakeskin pants and a scarf worn as a flimsy bikini to protect her nipples, who opposed the Kremlin while embodying the original "spirit of the October Revolution." In "The Living Sphinx of the Kamchatka Radioactive Volcano 1934" (above), she grapples with a giant mutated walrus, stuffing it into a volcano which blows it to smithereens. But it soon became apparent that Sadecky had concocted an elaborate scam by crudely doctoring parts of a proposed strip about an apolitical adventuress named Amazona by Czech artists Zdeněk Burian and Bohuslav Konečný to create anti-Soviet pop propaganda. Sadecky was exposed and sued, but he took the full truth to his grave when he died of a brain tumor in Germany in 1991. Regardless, Octobriana lives on as a cult icon. David Bowie wanted to cast Amanda Lear in a movie of her story, while Bryan Talbot was the first of several artists to use her as the heroine of new adventures.

OCTOBRIANA AND THE RUSSIAN UNDERGROUND, 1971, PUBLISHED BY TOM STACEY LTD., LONDON, 176-PAGE HARDBACK BOOK. WRITTEN BY PETR SADECKY AND DRAWN BY VARIOUS ARTISTS

Ильич

"EVERY TIME YOU LOOK INTO A MIRROR, REMEMBER IT WAS A WHITE MAN WHO HURT YOU!"

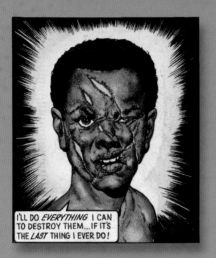

In British-occupied "Toganda" little Kruma sets off on his first trek to the Christian Mission. The African child has never seen a car or one of the white men who drive them, and is unaware that all Togandans must salute their racist rulers. His punishment is a brutal whipping which leaves him horribly disfigured and bent on revenge. After the British leave Toganda in 1960, the adult Kruma rises to become president, taking money from the communist Chinese, on condition that he removes all missionaries. Unknown to Kruma, the Chinese are also backing a rival, Zuloo, to take his place. It sounds like a job for The Crusaders. God always provides for this American black-and-white team of Jim Carter and Tim Emerson, Christian troubleshooters. Pray and a cheque arrives for their airfare. Quote from the Bible and Jim converts Zuloo. "Whitey" Tim only has to jump in front of Kruma and save him from a gunman for Kruma to see the light. After 40 years Jack Chick's "soul-winning" tracts continue to sell in their millions worldwide.

THE CRUSADERS NO. 3: SCAR FACE, 1974, PUBLISHED BY & © CHICK PUBLICATIONS, CHINO, CALIFORNIA, 36-PAGE COMIC. WRITTEN BY JACK T. CHICK, DRAWN BY FRED CARTER

THE
usaders
SCAR FACE
OL. 3
AAIIIEEEE! MY FACE!...IT ISN'T ME ANYMORE !

"I'M SORRY MEN, BUT THERE ARE NO MORE LIFEBELTS!"

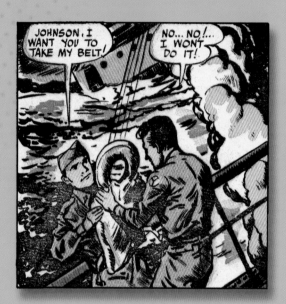

Four chaplains in uniform, looking remarkably tranquil as the ocean swallows them up, might make for a decidedly offbeat war-comic cover. In fact, the accompanying tale inside, "Bravery in the Heart," recounts the true story of how four chaplains from different faiths "willingly met death with prayers on their lips." Over four pages we see how they helped save many soldiers' lives when the US Army cargo troop transport *Dorchester* was torpedoed by the Nazis on February 3, 1943 in freezing waters off the coast of Greenland. Their final sacrifice is to give away their lifebelts to save others and then go down with the sinking ship. Theirs is only one of 16 short docu-comics on the heroism of priests in battle.

THE LIVING BIBLE NO. 3: CHAPLAINS AT WAR, SPRING 1946,
PUBLISHED BY & © THE LIVING BIBLE CORPORATION, NEW YORK,
52-PAGE COMIC. COVER BY L.B. COLE, INTERIOR STORIES AND ART UNCREDITED

CHAPLAINS
AT WAR
L.B.Cole
Bravery favors no religion ... bravery is in the heart!
THE LIVING BIBLE
10

"OTHERS HAVE GIT UP AND GIT -- YOU ONLY HAVE SIT DOWN AND SIT!"

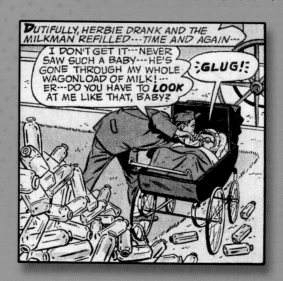

HERBIE

In his short black tie and round glasses, Herbie is a very fat, very slow boy of few words or emotions but numerous unexplained powers—walking in the air, talking to animals, traveling through time, indestructibility—some of them provided by his constant lollipops. Yet he's a disappointment to his egotistical failure of a father, Pincus Popnecker, who dismisses his son as a "little fat nothing." If only he knew that Herbie is one of the most extraordinary people on the planet. In this issue, Winston Churchill sends him in to subdue the Loch Ness monster. For his services in returning Nessie to the realm of the Unknown, Herbie is knighted by Queen Elizabeth. In another yarn, when he suspects the milkman of stealing the poorhouse fund his Dad has collected, Herbie disguises himself as a milk-guzzling baby. "The Fat Fury" is allegedly based on artist Ogden Whitney as a boy. The deadpan, sober clarity of his drawing, no matter how weird the stories get, makes them all the more unsettling. Some speculate that Herbie might be autistic or suffering from hallucinations.

HERBIE NO. 3, AUGUST 1963, PUBLISHED BY THE AMERICAN COMICS GROUP, NEW YORK, 36-PAGE COMIC. HERBIE IS © ROGER BROUGHTON/SWORD IN STONE PRODUCTIONS. WRITTEN BY "SHANE O'SHEA", ALIAS RICHARD HUGHES, DRAWN BY OGDEN WHITNEY

YOU WANT MORE? FATTIES 86 OUTSIDERS 100 DAIRY 62

№3
UGUST
IND.
MERICAN
MICS GROUP
ACG
MAKE WAY FOR the FAT FURY...
APPROVED BY THE COMICS CODE AUTHORITY
HERBIE
12¢
6
10d
OGDEN WHITNEY
H-HELP! W-WHAT ARE YOU GOING TO DO TO US, HERBIE?
YOU WANT I SHOULD BOP YOU WITH THIS HERE LOLLIPOP?

"LOOK WHAT HAPPENS TO A COCONUT WHEN BLASTED BY ONE OF THESE HI-SPEED HOLLOW-POINT BULLETS!"

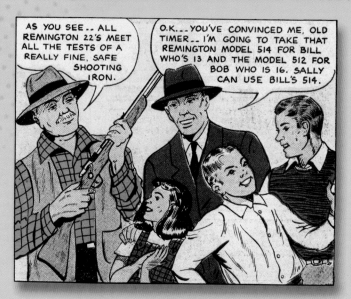

A jovial, pipe-smoking "old timer" is our host, who assures us that "Americans are naturally crack shots—all they need is a good gun and training" and offers "a lifetime of shooting fun" when you buy your kids one of Remington's five popular .22 rifles. On a visit to the gun store, Dad quickly chooses two models for his teenage boys and will let his youngest, Sally, use one of her brother's. After some tips on Remington's "Kleanbore" ammunition, it's time to make your own carnival-style shooting gallery with cut-out animal targets, "an electric motor and a little skill." While stressing safety and practice, the old timer promises the kids "a lot of sport, hunting small game and vermin such as rats, crows and rabbits." To many, the glazed smiles of those armed youngsters on the cover seem less reassuring 50 years on, in this post-Columbine era.

HOW TO SHOOT, 1952, PUBLISHED BY & © REMINGTON ARMS CO., BRIDGEPORT, CONNECTICUT, 16-PAGE FREE COMIC. WRITER AND ARTIST UNCREDITED

YOU WANT MORE?   FIREARMS 124   DEAR DADS 102   SPORTS 66

HOW TO SHOOT
GOOD EYES
GOOD SPORTSMANSHIP
GOOD HEALTH
GOOD FRIENDS
Remington RIFLES
HELPED BLAZE THE TRAIL
TO AMERICA'S GLORY
Remington
Serving American Sportsmen Since 1816"
DU PONT

"I SEE THIS TROPICAL CLIMATE MAKES THE MALES MUCH MORE HOT-BLOODED!"

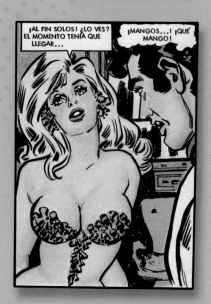

Ambitious Mexican movie muscleman Nacho spends half of this episode in nothing but his posing pouch as he is seduced by bikini-clad Russian blonde Olga Tigresova on her yacht at the Acapulco Film Festival. His big buddy Chéforo stays more level-headed, as clues point to Olga being involved in a secret Soviet operation. That night, Nacho goes to a premiere and meets Olga and other starlets in gorgeous, revealing outfits, although the arthouse European film puts him to sleep. Later, after narrowly escaping Bolshevik spies in a car chase, Nacho sneaks onto Olga's seemingly empty yacht, only to find her there, "more beautiful and suggestive than ever." Unable to resist her "mangos" he kisses her, but her lips have a strange bitter taste and he stumbles out, collapsing unconscious. Can you stand the suspense till next week?

LOS NOVIOS NO. 6, NOVEMBER 25, 1968, PUBLISHED BY & © AMERICA, CIA., MEXICO CITY, 28-PAGE COMIC. WRITTEN AND DRAWN BY MARIO GONZALEZ

YOU WANT MORE?   GORGEOUSNESS 98   ROMANCE 46   FASHIONS 44

LOS NOVIOS
SOLO PARA JOVENES...DE CUALQUIER EDAD
$1.00
totalmente a
COLORES SICODELICOS
BUSQUELA
LOS
"LUNES"

"THERE IS DEATH IN THAT PAW!"

KONA

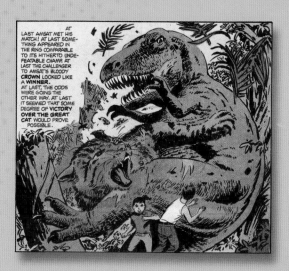

In story after story in this insanely hyperbolic serial, Kona, their white-maned Neanderthal ally, comes to the rescue of Dr. Dodd and his family, castaways on an uncharted monster-infested island. And those monsters don't come much stranger than Amsat, an abandoned kitten mutated by US nuclear test blasts and now 30-feet-high (years before TV's classic 1971 *Goodies* episode). When his deadly paw threatens little Lily and Mason, Amsat is briefly driven off by one of Kona's "pet tyrannosaurus." But that night, the fearsome feline's eyes glower at them from above the treetops, a constant menace. Kona and Dodd's solution is to use a wall of fire to drive the cat into the sea. There, Kona shoots him with an arrow laced with a paralyzing drug which Dodd has ground "from the timbo vine." Then with rabbit's blood Kona lures a large shoal of killer sharks. At first, Amsat feasts on the fish, but his gluttony and the sedative take their toll. Finally, with bits of the pussy's fur floating "like a dumped cargo of loose bearskins," what sinks are "only that great body's bones! These were all the shark left!" Peace never lasts long in this place, and for the cliffhanger Kona faces a truly gigantic sea serpent: "Great cat just little butterfly compared to this!"

KONA NO. 5, JANUARY—MARCH 1963, PUBLISHED BY & © DELL PUBLISHING CO., INC., NEW YORK, 36-PAGE COMIC. COVER BY VIC PREZIO, WRITTEN BY DON SEGALL, DRAWN BY SAM GLANZMAN

YOU WANT MORE?   DINOSAURS 104   GIANTS 110   RADIATION 8

ELL
2c
-398-303
N.—MAR.
KONA
MONARCH OF MONSTER ISL
PRIMITIVE WEAPONS
ARE THE ONLY HOPE!
CAN KONA DEFEAT
THE MONSTER CAT?

PS THE PREVENTIVE MAINTENANCE MONTHLY

"EYE-CHECK THE PARTS AS YOU HANDLE 'EM."

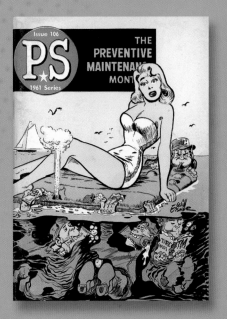

In 1942, Will Eisner, creator of *The Spirit*, was producing comics at the Pentagon for Army Motors magazine to show how troops should maintain their equipment. A study by the University of Chicago found that G.I.s read and retained much more from Eisner's plain-talking cartoon guides than regular dry technical manuals. No doubt they paid special attention to Connie Rodd, a pun on connector rod, his "gal mechanic, toothsome lass who operates the shop links, shortcuts, and cute tricks department." In 1951, Eisner got the same job on PS, as in "postscript," the Army's new "preventive maintenance monthly," and from Korea to Vietnam had Connie tease her all-male readers more than ever. So in "How To Strip Your Baby" from 1969's M16A1 Rifle guide, she purrs: "You want to know her inside out, every contour and curve, every need and whim, what makes her tick. No better time to get all-over acquainted than when you disassemble/assemble her for servicing." Before leaving in 1971, Eisner added the black, equally curvaceous Bonnie. Both tutors continue today but, as women make up around 15% of the U.S. Army, PS has to be more PC now.

PS THE PREVENTIVE MAINTENANCE MONTHLY, NOS. 106 AND 230, AUGUST 1961 & JANUARY 1972, PUBLISHED BY & © THE DEPARTMENT OF THE ARMY, FORT KNOX, KENTUCKY, 68-PAGE DIGEST-SIZED COMIC. WRITTEN AND DRAWN BY WILL EISNER AND AMERICAN VISUALS CORPORATION (NO.S 1—227), AND GRAPHIC SPECTRUM SYSTEMS (NO.S 228—251). CENTERFOLD PIN-UP BY CHUCK KRAMER

YOU WANT MORE?   MILITARY 58   FIREARMS 48   GORGEOUSNESS 80

HINDSIGHT PM IS COSTLY
GASOLINE IS NOT FOR CLEANING
PM IS FOR EVERYBODY
TEST THAT PART-KNOW BEFORE YOU THROW
BLOWS ENGINES
OVER REVVING
TWIST GENTLY
COMMO SWITCH
CARRY YOU GO WITH
EVERYTHING YOU GOT
A BUMMER
PM IS FOR REAL

"I'LL DO ANYTHING TO COMBAT THIS EVIL WE KNOW AS TERRORISM!"

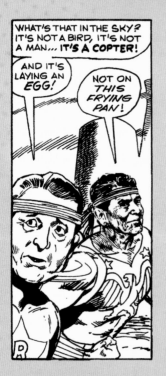

In this Eighties comic, Chernobyl was no accident but a failed terrorist plot. Now the same evil mastermind plans to make three American nuclear plants overheat to lethal meltdown. Determined to stop them no matter what, President Reagan decides to brave the still-experimental Alpha-Soldier process which "can turn an average body into that of a veritable superman." While this has killed younger test subjects, luckily it works better on "an older organism." So Reagan, 75 at the time, insists that Vice President George Bush, Secretary of Defense Caspar Weinberger and the rest of his senior cabinet join him. They are reborn as the equivalents of Captain America crossed with Rambo, gaining superpowered physiques as well as instant commando expertise, though it does nothing for their wrinkly faces. Littered with in-jokes from Reagan's movies, two more issues saw the cabinet busting cocaine suppliers in Bolivia and rescuing POWs from the Viet Nam jungle.

REAGAN'S RAIDERS NO.1, 1986, PUBLISHED BY & © SOLSON PUBLICATIONS, NEW YORK, 36-PAGE B/W COMIC. CREATED BY MONROE ARNOLD AND RICH BUCKLER, INTERIOR ART BY DICK AYERS, RICH BUCKLER AND JASON RODGERS

YOU WANT MORE?   WORLD LEADERS 22   SUPERHEROES 16   VIET NAM 78